Traditional Literatures
of the American Indian

Traditional Literatures of the American Indian
Texts and Interpretations

SECOND EDITION

COMPILED AND EDITED BY KARL KROEBER

UNIVERSITY OF NEBRASKA PRESS   LINCOLN AND LONDON

Dell H. Hymes, "Narrative Form as a 'Grammar'
of Experience: Native Americans and a Glimpse of
English," originally appeared in
Journal of Education 164, no. 2 (1982): 121–42.
Reprinted with permission.

∞ The paper in this book meets the minimum
requirements of American National Standard
for Information Sciences—Permanence of
Paper for Printed Library Materials, ANSI
z39.48-1984.
Library of Congress Cataloging-in-
Publication Data
Traditional literatures of the American Indian
  p.   cm.
ISBN 0-8032-2733-7 (cl: alk. paper).—ISBN
0-8032-7782-2 (pa: alk. paper)
1. Indian literature—United States—History and criticism.
2. Indian literature—United States—Translations into English.
PM151.T73   1997
810.9'897—dc20   96-23682
                                                          CIP

To the memory of my parents
Alfred Louis Kroeber, 1876–1960
Theodora Kroeber Quinn, 1897–1979

Contents

Acknowledgments

Grateful acknowledgment is made to *Western American Literature* for permission to reprint here Jarold Ramsey's essay, which originally appeared in that publication, and to the Columbia University Press and the University of Chicago Press for permission to use material quoted within that segment of this volume; to the Boston University *Journal of Education* for permission to reprint Dell Hymes's essay; and to Duke University Press for permission to reprint Linda Ainsworth's essay. The essay by Barre Toelken and Tacheeni Scott is based upon and expands Barre Toelken's "The 'Pretty Languages' of Yellowman: Genre, Mode, and Texture in Navajo Coyote Tales," which first appeared in *Genre* and is used here by permission of that journal. I am personally grateful to the Columbia University Press for permission to reproduce in this book's introduction the text and translation of "Red Willow." I am even more grateful to Patricia Sterling for her superb copyediting of the second edition.

Karl Kroeber

Traditional Literatures
of the American Indian

An Introduction to the Art
of Traditional American Indian
Storytelling

KARL KROEBER

This book offers a glimpse into the amazingly diversified body of oral narratives created by the first inhabitants of North America. Most of this Native American literature was destroyed—along with Indian peoples and their cultures—by European invaders following Columbus. Yet much has survived, and this volume's dozen stories only hint at the richness of artistic accomplishments of traditional Indian cultures—accomplishments being carried forward in new directions by contemporary Indian poets and novelists who have in the past quarter-century created a "Native American Literary Renaissance." [1]

The tales and accompanying commentaries printed here have been selected to suggest both the social range and emotional power of the artistic achievements of the first Americans. I have learned from teaching this material, however, that most people familiar only with Western writing are baffled by traditional Indian narratives. Occasionally there is a story with a theme so familiar, or a situation so dramatically structured, that a contemporary reader may respond to it with spontaneous pleasure and excitement: such a rarity is "Coyote and the Shadow People" in Jarold Ramsey's essay. But most Indian tales are not so accessible, and their strangeness is frustrating to readers who wish to gain something more than a superficial (and therefore patronizing) understanding of Indian storytelling.

It is also discouraging to learn that even though thousands of Indian stories have been preserved, they were all originally recited (and often recorded) in hundreds of different languages, for many of which there are neither grammars nor dictionaries and often no longer any native speakers. Our only access is through translations—frequently by anthropologists or folklorists without much literary skill—whose accuracy we have no way to check. We are faced, moreover, by double translation: not only the Englishing of a foreign language but also a *written* text representing an *oral* recitation, since none of the native peoples of North America depended on writing. Aside from these language problems, we must ask ourselves, is it possible to understand a story from a vanished culture of whose characteristics we are entirely ignorant? How can we comprehend a mythic narrative without having knowledge about the society in which it originated and whose beliefs and practices and forms of discourse the myth embodies?

Despite these daunting obstacles, it *is* possible to read traditional Indian stories with pleasure and profit. By surmounting the difficulties I have sketched, furthermore, we may learn some valuable lessons about how to respect what at first seems bafflingly alien. Being forced, for example, to recognize how badly prepared we are to understand Indian myths should compel us to recognize that we are never innocent and unprejudiced readers. We have been taught to read and respond in very specific ways to particular kinds of texts. We never react uninhibitedly to anything we read or hear. As a professional student of literature I can enable students to become aware of the unconscious prejudices they have learned only if I admit that I, too, lost my responsive innocence long ago. Even as a child I unabashedly "corrected" recitals to me of Yurok myths by Robert Spott, a full-blood Yurok who entertained me when I was bedridden. My "corrections" were based on earlier tellings by my anthropologist father. Exhibiting a sense of humor characteristic of most Indians, Robert was deeply amused at my childish firmness in insisting that he adhere exactly to what I claimed were "authentic" versions of his sacred myths.

Once we perceive that unconscious prejudice, as much as unfamiliarity, blocks our understanding of Indian stories, we may be able to make a simple but useful assumption: these tales are surprising because they are so artistically shaped. All carefully crafted literary works raise troubling problems, being composed of intricacies that both attract and defeat the most intense analytical intelligence—consider the history of *Hamlet*. The primary misconception we must abandon is that Indian stories are "primitive," in the sense of being artistically crude, rudimentary, undeveloped.

It may help us correct the misconception if we think of the lovely incised paintings of possibly twenty thousand years ago preserved in caves at Lascaux and Altamira and (perhaps the most wonderful yet) near Vallon Pont d'Arc, which no sensitive observer would dismiss as "primitive." If, analogously, we consider traditional Indian stories as requiring the most sophisticated critical analysis we can bring to bear, we will discover that many simple-seeming tales disclose beautifully articulated structures evocative of complex ideas and powerful emotions.

Alan Dundes, a distinguished folklorist and student of Indian storytelling, has exhorted his fellow scholars to recognize the "internal criteria" of three interacting "levels" that determine the significant forms of oral narrative. The first level is *texture,* or all the features of verbal form: sentences, words, even the phonemes making up the words. Second, *text* refers to a single telling of a tale. A text can be translated, but texture cannot, as Dundes illustrates with the proverb "Coffee boiled is coffee spoiled." One can easily enough imagine that text being translated, he observes, but it seems unlikely that the chief textural feature, the boiled-spoiled rhyme, would survive. Third, *context* is the specific social situation in which the story is told, "exactly how, when, where, to whom, and by whom the myth is uttered on a given specific occasion." [2]

Dundes distinguishes context, text, and texture because he believes that complete understanding of each oral story comes only from determining the special interrelations among the three aspects. Literary criticism, in fact, is the study of exactly these interrelationships, which when they have been carefully and consciously structured make up what we call a literary work of art. If we assume that Indian stories are not "primitive" but seem strange because organized by an artistry with which we are unfamiliar, we may be able to discover internal relations that illuminate the unfamiliar (perhaps extinct) culture within which the story originated.

Such criticism is hazardous and uncertain, but its rewards may be suggested by looking closely at some rather unostentatious narratives. Literary analysis of even so brief a piece as the Kato tale "The Man Eater" will highlight verbal features—details of texture—that a professional linguist might ignore. These problematic elements direct attention to possible purposes of the telling—issues of context—that an ethnologist probably would not notice. And the several meaningful uncertainties uncovered by analysis of this text suggest an adroit craftsmanship within this apparently artless tale.[3]

The Man Eater

be L	na t goot Lon	ya'nee.	Le ne'ha'	na nesh	in che'
Rope /	they were tying /	they say./	All /	persons /	deer/

on gee lang	ya'nee.	sah doong ha'	ts kaL	ya'nee.	t booL
went after /	they say. /	Alone /	she walked /	they say./	Basket/

ye geL	ya'nee.	toots	chh ghooL teeL	ya'nee.
she was carrying /	they say. /	Cane /	she walked with /	they say. /

t booL	tallon	chh geL	ya'nee.	"sheeye'	inche' "
Basket /	soft /	she carried /	they say. /	"My /	deer"

chh in   ya'nee.   chh eL choot   ya'nee.   noon shoos teeng
she said / they say. / She caught him /   they say. /   She took him up

t booL bee'   noL teeng   ch'tesgeeng   ya'nee.
basket in /   she put him /   she carried him /   they say.

choongkeebo isch   o ye tah   wa ge goosh   t booL
Tree bent down /   under places /   carrying through /   basket /

noon chh ooL gal'   ochhoonga   ya'nee.   chh geL   ya'nee yee dookh.
she whipped /   over it /   they say. / She carried / they say / up hill./

choong   oo yey   wa oong nging   choong   yeeL choot.
Tree /   under /   she carried through /   tree /   he caught. /

da kit dool boosh.   woong ha   na goot daL   yee dookh.
He embraced it. /   Anyhow /   she went on /   up hill. /

noon chhooL gal'   toots   booL.   tshkon nes ne chhin   ya'nee.
She whipped /   cane /   with. /   She found out / she said (?) / they say./

na gool dal   hai da oong.   "sheeye'   inche'   tachee? "
She ran back /   down hill. /   "My /   deer /   where? " /

chhin   ya'nee.   deena nesh   da bes ya   choon khwoot.
she said / they say. / This man /   climbed on /   tree on. /

Loosh dee cho   chh ghooL tal   ya'nee.   sha   kasyai   ya'nee.
Rotten log /   she kicked /   they say. / Sun / came up / they say. /

the'   kwna'   oo chhoong a   naL chos   ya'nee.
Blanket / her eyes /   over them /   she put /   they say. /

nee   ka no t yan   na heL'oots   ya'nee.   hai dookh   ya'nee.
She was ashamed. / She ran back /   they say / here up /   they say. /

kwoon Lang.
All. /

Free Version

They were setting snares for deer. All the people had gone after deer. He was walking alone. Some one was carrying a burden-basket. She was walking along with a cane. She was carrying a soft burden-basket.

"My deer," she said. She caught him and put him in the basket. She carried him off. When she had to carry the basket under the branches of trees she whipped over her shoulder with her cane. She went east up the hill. When she went under a tree, he caught it and climbed up on it. She went on just the same, whipping with her cane. She found out what had happened. She ran back down the hill.

"Where is my deer?" she said.

The man climbed the tree. She kicked against a rotten log thinking he might be under it. The sun came up. She covered her face with her blanket because she was ashamed and ran up here east.

That is all.

The difference between the translator's literal, interlinear and his free translation allows us to perceive how verbal problems may open a way into critical analysis. Notice, for instance, the omission of "they say" (*ya'nee*) from the translator's free version. In all the other Kato myths this translator collected, however, except in the one story of a personal experience he transcribed, *ya'nee* appears frequently. It is reasonable to assume that for the Kato teller *ya'nee* is a signal implying something like "This is not *my* story, not a personal report, but a traditional myth." But why should *ya'nee*, "they say," be repeated so often?

One answer may be that *ya'nee* is also used as a structural marker. It concludes each of the first ten sentences of "The Man Eater." In the eleventh *ya'nee* for the first time appears in mid-sentence, and then disappears as the man escapes—until the monster discovers her loss and again when she speaks a second time. *Ya'nee* then concludes each of the final five sentences except the penultimate one, perhaps because it occurs both in the middle and at the end of the last sentence. This formulaic element, then, only twice interrupts sentences, at the halfway point, just before the captured man escapes as the monster strides off triumphantly slashing tree branches, and at the end when she retreats in shamed defeat. Such placings (accompanying the recitalist's closer association of *ya'nee* with monster than with man) illustrate how a textural feature may shape text structure, the double functioning allowing a nonexpert to recognize the story's meaningfully constructed form.

Also notable is the discrepancy in the translator's two versions of the third sentence, the interlinear "Alone *she* walked" differing from the free version's "*He* was walking alone." Can one imagine a Kato teller or Kato listener confusing the monster and her victim? Probably not, yet the discrepancy calls attention to a pervading theme of isolation in the story. Was the man captured because he separated himself from the group hunt emphasized in sentences one and two? Is the man eater's "monstrosity" her aloneness? One cannot answer simply and definitively because of the intense compression of the story: not only is it brief, but it is made up of less than fifty distinct words. One must attend as carefully to its verbal nuances as to those of a lyric poem in our literature. Each word, and its placing, seems chosen with great care, so that every interrelation of text and texture functions within dense patternings of diverse kinds. That manifold density, like the verbal richness of our lyric poetry, offers us the lasting pleasure of constant reinterpretation.

The emphasized parallelism in the monster's two speeches—when she finds and captures the man and after she discovers his escape—dramatically reinforces the story's fundamental narrative inversion, the hunter become the hunted, which helps to articulate the theme of isolate versus group. One can illustrate the interplay of verbal and thematic features by the "up-down" and "hard-soft" elements. The tale begins with snares of woven rope for deer; then a cane-carrying monster lifts the man up and drops him down into her woven back-basket, beating down tree branches with her cane until he escapes up a tree trunk. Discovering his loss on a hill, she rushes back down, vainly seeking him under a fallen, rotten tree. The sun rises up, exposing her shame, and raising her blanket over her face, she hastens off uphill.

These patterns are strengthened and complicated by aural echoings and inversions. The soft, horizontal log the monster kicks (*chh ghooL tal*) where the man is *not* hidden, aurally may recall her entrance with her hard cane (*chh ghooL teeL*), with which she twice whips (*noon chh ooL gal'*) the down-bending trees whose branches the man uses to flee from her. Analogously, the last sentence's final nonformulaic word, *hai dookh,* echoes the endings of pivotal sentences eleven and fourteen, *yee dookh.*

These comments are not intended to limit the context of "The Man Eater" by imposing a single interpretation on it. I suggest, instead, that like many Indian myths this story is interestingly complex, not easy to explain, because it is a crafted artifact. We can usefully apply to a narrative with so many "poetic" features the same kind of critical analyses we use to enrich our understanding of Western literary works. When one analyzes "The Man Eater" critically, one realizes that diverse interpretations of it are possible just *because* it is so artistically wrought. Even my few comments raise the possibility, for example, that this tale of a hunter hunted may be saying something about gender relations: it seems far from accidental that the "man eater" is a female equipped with both a cane and a uteruslike basket. Critical appreciation of the story, therefore, may give us insights into Kato culture that might not be brought to light through usual ethnographic techniques. Anthropologists lament that in matters such as gender relationships, understanding a different culture is extremely difficult because formalized social "regulations" so often conceal the complexity of truly decisive underlying attitudes. By regarding a story such as "The Man Eater" as artistically shaped to explore from the inside, as it were, a particular sociocultural set of behaviors and beliefs tied to gender relationships, we may gain insight into some dynamics of Kato culture as a vital practice.

We must not forget that critical judgments of literary works of Western culture are properly always tentative and subject to revision. Much of the critical energy expended on the plays of Euripides, the romances of Chrétien de Troyes, or the novels of James Joyce, for example, focuses on text-texture *problems* to establish what are only hypotheses about each work's link to its sociocultural context. Good critics of these works never claim complete understanding. By constructing possible relations between the context of a particular text based on analysis of texture, we may improve and extend appreciation of the works and the environment out of which they emerged, but we never attain definitive readings. The same investigative process is as appropriate and rewarding for Indian oral myths, although usually we must start with the most basic details because Indian narratives lack the history of earlier studies with which Western literary works are encrusted. It is our scholarship, not Indian storytelling, that is primitive, undeveloped.

Perhaps nothing is harder for us to appreciate, in our hypervisual, print-oriented society, than the experience of language by peoples without writing. All their ideas, feelings, beliefs, and imaginings are kept alive only by talking to one another and by listening attentively to what others say. To people for whom words exist only as sound, dying away even as spoken, verbal comment on the phenomena of the surrounding world and engagement in the special practices of their culture must be more ongoingly dynamic and dramatic than for us. Speaking is always a vital event, for spoken words are evanescent movements in time without the thinglike permanence of written words. In societies without writing, not only every story but also every speech is a realizing, a making real, of a particular culture. In such societies nothing is more important than words spoken and words heard, because each singular human way of life exists primarily through these utterances. Nothing should surprise us less than the unflagging care and attention to language by peoples who do not use writing. We would be wise to suspect that peoples without writing are consistently at least as careful as we are in structuring, in nuancing, and in weighing the diversity of effects produced by crafted utterances such as stories. It would be surprising indeed if nonwriting cultures did not possess a high degree of verbal artistry, yet one for which our print-oriented sensibilities and preconceptions leave us unprepared.

Because oral cultures exist and persist primarily through the stories people tell one another, the range of narratives in Native American societies is enormous. But one fundamental reason for storytelling has always been entertainment and enjoyment—it is a way to have fun, above all to laugh at others and at oneself—and a majority of traditional American Indian stories are funny stories, like this one told by a Creek Indian.[4]

The Fawn, the Wolves, and the Terrapin

A beautiful Fawn met a Wolf one day who asked how he came to have such pretty spots over his body. "I got under a sieve and they put fire over it, and that made the pretty spots."

"Will you show me how I can do that?" asked the Wolf. The Fawn consented. Then the Wolf obtained a large sieve and lay down under it, and the Fawn built a fire and burned him to death. After the flesh had decayed, the Fawn took the bones of the back and made a necklace of them. One day the Fawn met a pack of Wolves, who said to him, "Where did you get that necklace?" But he refused to tell. "What is the song we hear you singing as you gallop over the prairie?" asked the Wolves. "If you will stand here till I get to the top of yonder hill I will sing it for you."

Ya-ha ya-ha	Wolf, wolf
Ef-oo-ne-tul	bones only
Chesarsook, chesarsook	rattle, rattle
Chesarsook	rattle
Kah-ke-tul	The ravens only
Methl-methl	fluttered, fluttered
Soolee-tul	The buzzard only
Methl-methl	fluttered, fluttered
Charnur-tul	The flies only
Sum-sum	buzzed, buzzed
Choon-tah-tul	The worms only
Witter-took	wiggled
Witter-took	wiggled
Witter-took.	wiggled.

When the Wolves heard this song they howled in anger and said: "We missed our mate. He is dead and those are his bones. Let us kill his murderer."

They started for the Fawn, who, seeing them, sped away for life, the bones rattling as he ran. He came to a basket maker and begged him to place him under a basket, but he refused. Then the Fawn came to a man who was getting bark to cover his house. "Oh, hide me from the Wolves," he begged, but the man would not. He ran on and came to a Terrapin who was making a spoon. "Tell me where to hide from the Wolves," said the Fawn. "No," replied the Terrapin, "I must not take sides." However, the Fawn saw a stream just ahead, and on reaching it he jumped up and lodged in the fork of a tree and could not extricate himself.

The Wolves passed the man who was making baskets and the man who was getting bark to cover his house and came to the Terrapin, who told them the way Fawn had gone.

When the Wolves reached the stream, they could trace the Fawn no farther. They looked in the water, and there they saw him. They tried to go into the water to catch the Fawn but failed. In sorrow they began to howl. As they raised their heads in howling, they saw the Fawn in the tree. One Wolf said, "I know a man who can shoot him out"; so he sent for the man. Then he went to the Terrapin and brought him, and the Terrapin said he could kill him. He began to shoot arrows at the Fawn. He shot every arrow away and missed the Fawn. Afterwards, while walking around the tree, Terrapin found one of his old arrows sticking in the ground near an old log. "This was one of my best arrows," said he. So he shot at the Fawn and with this old arrow killed him.

Then the Wolves took the body and divided it into pieces. "We must pay the man for shooting him," one said, so they offered the Terrapin a piece of one leg. But he had some complaint in his leg, and the medicine men had told him not to eat the leg of any animal. He whined out, "I cannot eat leg; it will make my leg hurt, and I shall die."

When they offered him a shoulder, he whined out, "I cannot eat shoulder; it will pain my shoulder, and I shall die."

"He does not want any," they said, and went away carrying all of the Fawn.

After they had gone, the Terrapin looked around and saw that there was blood on the leaves; so he gathered the bloody leaves into a big bundle, saying, "I'll carry them home." He reached his house, threw down the bundle, and said to his wife, "There, cook it for the children." Then she unrolled the bundle but saw nothing. "Where is it?" she asked. "Way inside," replied he; so she separated the leaves, but finding nothing but blood, she threw it in his face. He called to the children to bring him some water; but as they were slow, he crawled around with his eyes closed and found the lye and washed his face in that. Some of this got in his eyes and made them red, and ever since terrapins have had red eyes.

Although John Swanton, who published this story, does not provide the original language, he does give a transliteration of the Creek for the Fawn's song, which is markedly onomatopoetic: even to Western ears *methl-methl* and *sum-sum* may sound like fluttering wings and buzzing flies. This light-hearted imitativeness may justify the suggestion that *witter-took* humorously "imitates" worm sounds. Yet the song is in its way rather formally ordered.

After the jeering *ya-ha ya-ha* address to the Wolves, the sound of the bones, whose tripled rattle rhymes with the worms' tripled wriggling, is succeeded by three doublets interlinked by the rhymed *tul*. It seems a reasonable guess that the surrounding tale may similarly exploit verbal playfulness through formal structuring to attain equivalently amusing effects.

Even in translation it is plain that the story emphasizes a theme of the fooling fool fooled. Credulous, envious Wolf gets himself burned to a crisp. His victimizer, Fawn, achieves a good start on Wolf's brothers, although Fawn can't resist either an appeal to his good looks or an opportunity for a taunting brag—quite in accord with his vanity in flaunting the doubly fatal necklace. Fawn stupidly (and absurdly) catches himself in a tree. Witlessly plunging after his image (reflecting Fawn's vanity?), the Wolves howl in frustration, and in raising their heads accidentally discover self-trapped Fawn. In keeping with their foolishness, they solicit the assistance of the worst incompetent available. Terrapin's vanity has less basis in fact than Fawn's, but by the improbable chance of finding a long-lost (so presumably crooked) arrow, he does finally kill Fawn for the inept Wolves. Then, greedily trying to scrounge more of the carcass than he's offered, Terrapin does himself out of any food at all. Here the narrative turns to domestic comedy, with Terrapin's attempt to impose on his wife earning him a faceful of bloody leaves. His error with the lye gets him the permanent discomfort of red eyes, a fitting conclusion to a tale beginning with a wolf seeing spots.

No laborious analysis is needed for this quick-moving narrative, with its humor varying from the slapstick of leaves-in-the-face to the sly contrast between dishonest Terrapin and the hard-working house-roofer and basket-maker. Yet we should not overlook the skill with which the listener is carried forward from the Fawn-Wolf rivalry to Terrapin as the useless paterfamilias, self-deceiving and finally self-injuring, so as to recall the Wolf's (and Fawn's) earlier self-destructions. The circularity of the tale thus appears condensed into the circularity of Fawn's song, and it seems certain that recognition of these formalized patternings is intended as one source of audience enjoyment. Such deft internal echoings reinforce the tale's genially sardonic "message": this is a world well supplied with vain and greedy fools. The easy skill of the narration fits with this broadly humane morality and surely reveals something about the quality of the people who enjoyed telling and listening to such a story; these were not morose savages dully killing time around a smoky fire.

It is not easy, in fact, to find in Western literature anything superior to the brilliantly economical characterization of Terrapin, a familiar braggart-liar type who in trying to cheat everyone else ends up bankrupting himself. Whatever the particular circumstances in which "The Fawn, the Wolves, and the Terrapin" was originally told, and whatever riches of its original texture have vanished in translation, even the English text offers pleasures to anyone willing to take satisfaction in a well-made verbal artifact reminding us of the unendingly repetitive absurdities of human behavior—pleasures that may recall Chaucer's equally unprimitive art in, say, "The Miller's Tale."

Yet even if we find "The Fawn, the Wolves, and the Terrapin" enjoyable, and recognize the society that created and retold it as far from unsophisticated, we may be reluctant to admit that oral art can manifest anything like the self-consciousness that distinguishes Western literature. The essays collected in this volume, however, demonstrate an impressive capacity for self-analysis among Native American storytellers and audiences. Misunderstanding of this point arises principally from our rigid and reductive ideas about the functions of narratives, especially mythic narratives, in oral cultures.

The unfortunately mind-boggling number of definitions of myth are often contradictory, but most agree on one point: myths are stories. So instead of fretting about how to define myth, let us consider the equally fundamental question, what is a story and what does it do?[5]

A story is a social transaction. Somebody tells somebody else about some events that provoke a judgmental response, even if that is only "Wow!" or "You're kidding!" Stories enable audiences to join with storytellers in assessing the significance of what they tell. A story does not exist without a response to it, because it is a social, not a private, event. Stories are meeting places; they are the discourse of encounter. What stories primarily do is enable people together to make sense (rational sense, humorous sense, religious sense) of contingencies ("a funny thing happened . . .") without eliminating the accidental quality of what has happened or might happen. Stories enable us to understand without fitting our perceptions to some abstract system of explanation. They are, consequently, the favorite human discourse for *exploring* the practices and beliefs that make up the cultural context shared by storytellers and their audiences. A Nez Percé tale illustrates how narrative can thus function as a psychosocial self-questioning process.[6]

píplaats
Red Willow

kaálaa	awáka	laáwtiwaa	hatá'aw	ta'áXatoom.
Just /	it was his /	comrade /	very dear /	a youth's. /

timaáy   hiwákaa.   kawó'   yoq' opí   timaáy   hiwáyatoo.
A maiden / she was. / Then /   that / maiden / went in quest of a vision. /

"poótimt   láhayn   koósa   kaa ts'aalwí   wát'oo'
"Ten /   days / I am going / and / if /   not /

paáytoqo'   a   nakoó'   waáqo'   koo'itoónm   póptsiown."
I return / you / will think / already /   something /   kills her." /

mát'oo   kii   oos   táwtiwa.   Kaawó'   hiwi'nana   kaa
But /   here / hers is / fiancé. /   Then /   she went /   and /

pátwixna   ta'áxatoom.   pátwixna   kaa   konaá   póptsiaawnaa
he followed her / the youth. / He followed her / and / there / he killed her /

ta'áxatoom.   waliímtsaapki   pá'wiya.   wát'oo'   mína
the youth. /   With an arrow /   he shot her. /   Not /   anywhere /

paánixqaanaa   tsápna.   pásapalooxqaanaa   kaa   hikóqaanaa
could he put /   the arrow. /   He would hide it /   and /   go away /

kaa   koónk'oo'   paáxnaaqaanaa   kaálaa   xaa'aáw   hilaaXaáwtsaa
and /   always /   he would see it / just /   a red glow / burning red /

íska   kiká't.   óykaakaapaa / hisapaloóka   mát'oo   koónk'oo'
like /   blood. /   At all places / he hid it /   but /   always /

paáxnaaqaanaa   kaálaa   hilaaxaá'aawtsaa.   konaá   hihína,
he would see it /   just /   glowing red. /   There /   he said, /

"iyó!   taamaawiín.   mínax   aawnikaáX? "   kiímat   kaa
"Confound it! / It is too much. / Where / shall I put it? " /   When /   then

konmaá   pawstooka'áyka   tsápna   kaa   konó'
over that way / he shot it /   the arrow / and / there

hitqapalakapaya   píplaatspaa.   kaa   wát'oo'   mína   páxna
it stuck amid /   willows. /   And /   not / anywhere / he saw it. /

kii   kaawó'   hitskilíyna   kaa   konaá   hiwíynaaqaanaa,
Now / then /   he went home / and / there /   he would weep, /

"iínim   ootáwtiwa,   iínim   ootáwtiwa."   kaa   ipnátsa,
"My /   fiancée, /   my /   fiancée." /   And / saying to himself, /

NEBRASKA

University of Nebraska Press
312 North 14th Street
Lincoln, NE 68588-0484
(402) 472-3581

Please accept this review copy with the compliments of the author and the publisher. We request that you send two copies of your published review.

Name of publication: *Traditional Literatures of the American Indian: Texts and Interpretations* **(Second Edition)**

Compiled and edited by Karl Kroeber

Publication date: April 11, 1997

Cloth price: $35.00

Paper price: $12.00

"mii'sax   hipaamaáynaaX,   ipním   póptsiaawnaa."
"How could it be of me / they would suspect me, / that he / killed her." /

ku'ús hiwanípa,   kaálaa   hiwíytsa.   kaa   oos   aásqaap,
Thus / he sang, /   just /   he is weeping. / And / his is / younger brother, /

kaálaa   hiXaláwisa,   ipnaataamqitaayítsaa   tsápki   kaa
just /   he plays /   spearing targets /   with arrows /   and /

hiwanpís   ipínk'oo',   "iínim   ootáwtiwa,   iínim   ootáwtiwa."
he sings /   he, too, /   "My /   fiancée, /   my /   fiancée." /

kii ipnaatXtaayítsaa   kaa   pikápim   pána,   "maanaámaa
Here / he spears targets /   and / his mother / said to him, / "What is

yoX   ku'ús   hitátoo?"   "kaálaa naa'yaátsaap   aamts'iítaato
that /   thus / you keep saying?" / "Just / my elder brother / I often hear

hiwanptátoo   kaa   kaálaa   asapálapsqooyasa."   pikápim
he sings often /   and / just / I am imitating him." /   His mother /

kii   pána   pisítna,   "waáqo' paays   áta   póptsiaawnaa."
here / said to him / the father, / "Now / probably / it is that / he killed her." /

átka   waáqo   hikóqaanaa   poótimt   láhayn;   kaa   waáqo
Because / now / he would go /   ten /   days /   and /   now /

timaáynim   píka   hiwíynima.   kaa   hilaXsáXtsa, hisaayóXo'saa
the maiden's / mother / wept. /   And / opens wide her mouth, /   looks /

maqsámkinkayx   ka   konmá   akoóya   paáhaap.   (áta
toward the mountain / that which / way / hers went / daughter. / (It was that

ta'áxatoom   kaakaá   póptsiaawnaa,   timaáyina   hoókux
the youth /   when /   he killed her, /   the maiden's /   hair /

paasaak'iíwkaa'nyaa   kaa   yoq' opí   hinápta   kaakaá   hiwanpísa,
he had cut hers off /   and / that /   he holds / while /   he sings,

ha'átXawtsa   mat   hitilaáptsaa.) kaawó' hiwíynima   aátwaay,
deeply grieves / but also / longs.) / Then / she wept /   the old woman, /

kii / ku'ús   hiXsáxtsa   hiwíytsa.   kiímat   tsilyáxnim
like / this / she opens wide her mouth / she weeps. / Thereupon /   a fly

q'o'   ts'aa'aá'   him   poóyayalaka'nya   kaa   q'o'
precisely / true /   her mouth /   it flew into /   and / at once /

pátqakanpa   tsilyáxna   ——   t'uks   q'o'   tsilyáxna;
she bit it /   the fly /   ——   burst open / thereupon / the fly; /

isiímat   maátsi'n,   kaa   ipnána   aátwaay,   "waá'qu'
behold /   fetid, /   and / she said to herself / the old woman, / "Already /

átax   ti'nxniín   was   miyaá'ts." kaawó'   pá'pawisana
it is that mine / dead /   is /   child." /   Then / they searched for her /

timaáyinaa   átka   waáqo'   aátwaaynim   oýkaalonaa   hinásna,
the maiden / because /   now /   the old woman / all of them / said to them, /

"ti'nxniín   hiíwas."   kaa   hipakoóya   maqsámkax
"Dead /   she is." /   And /   they went /   to the mountains

pá'pawisana.   kaawó'   kii   paáyaaXtsaanaa.   áta   inakiíx
looking for her. /   Then /   here /   they found her. / It was that /   even

pawawiíka   mát'oo   paáyaaXtsaanaa   kaa   páxtsana   áta
he had buried her / but /   they found her /   and /   they saw /   that /

awyiín   hiíwas,   kaa   pá pawisana   itoóki   pá'awya.
shot /   she is, /   and /   they searched for that / with which / he had shot her. /

q'o'   tsaáyaa   tsap   mína.   óykaaslix   hipaasaayóXo'yaa,
Absolutely / absent / arrow / anywhere. / All about /   they searched, /

q'o'   wát'oo'   maáwaa   tsápna   paáyaaXtsaanaa.   kii
absolutely / not /   ever /   the arrow /   they found. /   Here /

hipanáx tsixliyka   tsilaáxt   kaa   konaá   patamiksána   kaa
they took home /   the body /   and /   there /   they buried her / and /

wát'oo'   maáwaa   hipatsoóxwana   isiínm   póptsiaawnaa,
not /   ever /   they found out /   who /   killed her /

átka   wát'oo'   tsap   paáyaaXnaaysaanaa.   konix   hiwts'áya
because /   not /   arrow /   they found his. / From there / it became /

píplaats   ilp'ílp,   timaáynim   kikát.
willow /   red, /   the maiden's /   blood. /

Free Translation

A youth had a very dear comrade (and fiancée)—a maiden. It came to pass that the maiden went in quest of a vision. "I am going for ten days, and if I do not return, then you will know that something has killed me." Here was her fiancé, and when she went this youth followed her. He followed and killed her; shot her with an arrow. He could find no place to put the arrow. He tried to hide it, but always on going away he could see it glowing red, glowing like blood. He hid it in many places, but always he would see the red glow. There he said to himself, "Confound it! This is too much. Where shall I place it?" Thereupon he shot the arrow away and it stuck amid willows, and he saw it no more. Now he went home. There he began to weep, "My fiancée, my fiancée." But to himself he would say, "How could they suspect me of killing her?" Thus he sang and wept. He had a younger brother who played about, spearing targets with arrows; and he, too, now began to sing, "My fiancée, my fiancée." Here he was spearing targets when his mother said to him, "What is this you say constantly?" — "I am only imitating my elder brother; I hear him sing often." The mother now said to his father, "It is likely that he has killed her." They had noticed, also, that he would go away for ten-day periods. Now the maiden's mother wept, opening wide her mouth, and looked toward the mountain to which her daughter had gone. (It was that when the youth had killed the maiden, he had cut off her hair; and this hair he clutched as he sang, deeply grieving and longing.) The old woman, the maiden's mother, wept. She wept with her mouth open, and a fly flew directly into it. She bit down on the fly quickly and burst it open; behold, the fly was fetid. She said to herself, "My child is already dead." Then a search was made for the maiden because the old woman had announced, "She is dead." They went to the mountains to search for the body. There they found it where he had even tried to bury the maiden; they found her and saw that she had been shot. They searched for the arrow with which she had been shot, but there was none to be found. They searched all about, but never did they find the arrow. They took the maiden's body home and buried it there. They never found out who had killed her because the arrow was never found. From that it came to pass that the willow is red—of the maiden's blood.

The obvious question posed by this tale is why the young man killed his fiancée. We are tempted to answer by speculating about the possible relevance of tribal customs, taboos, special rites. We expect the answer from anthropological information. In this case I have looked into the ethnological data but have found only that the maiden's quest for a guardian spirit involved going alone into a wilderness area and fasting and praying that some animal spirit would appear in a vision—a major religious practice of the Nez Percés (as well as many other Indian peoples). I have found no comment on an event such as the one described in "Red Willow."

Is it unreasonable to think the man's action may have been to the Nez Percés themselves mysterious? Is it not possible that dramatizing a puzzle of motive may have been a purpose of this story? After all, the presentation of the mystery of motive has a long history in Western literature; think once more of *Hamlet*. By foregrounding the *unanswered* question of why the youth kills his fiancée, the Nez Percé storyteller compels the members of his audience to confront with him the dark uncertainties in the heart of each. For me, at any rate, this possibility is strengthened by the fact that critical analysis founded on that hypothesis illuminates several details in the story whose significance otherwise remains murky.

A literary critic is bound to be struck, for example, by the fact that there is no way of being certain *to* whom the maiden speaks in the fourth sentence. Then one notices that who is (or is not) addressed seems important throughout the story. Thus the murderer and his victim's mother both speak to themselves. This seems appropriate for the murderer, since he appears to be a divided personality. Yet his private lamentation is meant to deceive the tribal group, although, ironically, the echo of his words by his younger brother crystallizes his mother's suspicion—which she voices only to the killer's father, not the tribe. The maiden's mother first speaks to herself, then addresses the tribe, sending them out to find her daughter's body but not the identity of her killer. These contrasting parallelisms work to develop other ironies. The murderer remains undetected because the fatal weapon is not located, even though the natural world continues to "proclaim" its place of concealment through the red of the willow plant—just as the traditional story itself continues to "disclose" what was unknown with certainty to the tribal group. "Red Willow" is, in both the most obvious and most subtle senses, the disclosure of a mystery.

The more we examine the story, the more we perceive the interplay of concealment and revelation fulfilling this paradoxical purpose. The tribe fails to discover the murderer, although this traditional story identifies him as its anonymous protagonist. That anonymity, implying that the killer might be *anyone,* suggests why we have difficulty recognizing his motive. We may be hesitant to admit a grim impulse not unknown in our own hearts. About such impulses we desire to deceive ourselves, just as the youth deceives himself when he exults that his lamentations make invisible his criminality: "How could they suspect me of killing her?" His misleading mourning may express a true anguish he conceals from himself, evidenced by the hair he cut from the girl's head and kept. Through his compulsive reenactment of his fiancée's quest, he grieves for the loss of what he made to disappear, surely a psychological paradox that is, alas, all too familiar. As the killer tries to hold on to what he destroyed, his younger brother's "playing" — that is, shooting at a target rather than at real *game* — unwittingly betrays the crime to their parents. We may have difficulty in explaining the psychic process by which the echoed lament precipitates belief of guilt in his mother's mind, but the repeated conjunction of the words "my fiancée, my fiancée" just as the arrow plunges into its target might initiate an unprovable yet certain intuition — especially if in her mind there had previously lurked a suspicion too terrible to admit.

These psychological details show "Red Willow" to be a story subtly crafted to enable its audience to examine self-concealed impulses. The younger brother's "reflecting" the elder's action, for example, is reinforced by interlocked rhetorical and linguistic patterns. One of the most interesting is the word *kaálaa,* which Phinney translates interlinearly as "just" but omits from the free translation, perhaps because the word's function is more rhetorical than semantic. After opening the story, the word recurs in sentences ten and eleven, when the murderer can find no place to hide the deadly arrow; again when he weeps just before the younger brother appears; and then as the introductory element of the two clauses of the younger brother's unconsciously revealing repetitions as his arrows strike home.

Another effective rhetorical device is the intruding of the killer's false/true grieving into the midst of the mother's lament, because the interruption reinforces the ironic linkage of these "opposed" sorrows. Adroitly placed also is *kii,* which is usually translated as "here" but would seem more accurately rendered in English by "now," because it always points up a critical *moment* of action or revelation — as when the reburial of the girl marks the tribe's definitive failure to discover her murderer. The putrid fly that shoots "precisely true," *q'o ts'aa'aá',* into the mother's mouth from the mountain (thus revealing the daughter's first burial place) is inversely echoed by the "absolutely absent," *q'o tsaáyaa,* arrow — which *could* have solved the mystery. The foul insect in the mother's mouth thus "speaks" not only to the place and condition of the girl's body but also to the corruption in the man who is simultaneously her lover and her killer.

This artistry is needed because the story itself articulates what is difficult to talk about openly, difficult even for one to think about to oneself. The narrative does not merely illustrate a conventionalized attitude toward a problem of social relationships; it does more than restate a conventional taboo. It explores and dramatizes the tensions out of which arise patterned cultural attitudes, beliefs, and practices. This is a major function of myths for the Indians as is literature for us: to allow us to face up to the ferocious and painful impulses, both psychological and social, that cultural formations are created to channel, control, and direct. So long as we think of Indian myths as merely representing sociocultural practices already in place, the stories as mere products, we won't understand them and will be tempted to dismiss them as puzzling or trivial. Only when we recognize that like our own best literary art they embody testings, examinations, questionings of cultural practices and assessments of the values and costs of socially defined constraints and freedoms will we begin to appreciate them as dynamic processes upon which the persistence and vital transformativeness of oral societies primarily depend.

The vision quest on which the girl in "Red Willow" sets out is, anthropologists tell us, central to Nez Percé religion.[7] I have found no ethnographic discussion of what sometimes must have occurred in the dangerous circumstances of those quests, possibilities to which "Red Willow" speaks with such troubling poignancy. The myth articulates in psychologically and socially efficacious fashion deep psychic tensions that necessarily derive from this intense search for supernatural aid. In no way does this exploration into the shadowed aspects of the vision quest undermine the Nez Percé religion. To the contrary, the story proves that these Indians did not conceal from themselves the psychological dangers of the vision quest—dangers about which Western ethnologists have been silent. Even more specifically, the story dramatizes the destructive force of psychological impulses which it is the successful guardian spirits' function to reorient into constructive channels, for both individual and tribal group. We need knowledge of Nez Percé religion to understand "Red Willow," but we need also to recognize that the artistry of the story is deployed to give the Nez Percés insight into the fundamental dynamics out of which they constructed their culture, painful and difficult as that insight might be. If we wish to appreciate Native American cultures fully, we must learn to do justice to the verbal skillfulness that helps to sustain those cultures as dynamic practices.

The essays in this volume have been chosen to allow nonspecialist readers some insight into the range of Indian oral artistry as well as into recently developed techniques for translating and critically interpreting this material. In the first essay Jarold Ramsey sensitively describes the devices of symmetrical structuring, prefiguration, and intensely focused dramatic speech and gesture to explain how the Nez Percé recitalist evokes a poignancy unsurpassed by any of the thousands of other Orpheus stories from around the world. The device of prefiguring deserves special comment, because that device, not suspense, characterizes most Indian storytelling. To each Indian people its myths were at least as familiar as biblical stories are to us. Because the Indian audience knew in broad outline "what was going to happen next," storytellers used prefigurative rather than suspenseful narration to bring into awareness subtle and unexpected meanings in familiar tales, thereby calling forth more imaginative response in their listeners.

Ramsey deftly compares the brilliant artistry of the Nez Percé story with two parallel tales (which I append to his essay) from other tribal groups, displaying how each is built around a different but equally valuable dramatizing of human frailities and desires. Using these comparisons to define the unique quality of the Nez Percé myth, Ramsey points out how in its surprising final episode the narrative seems to move even beyond the modes and logic of myth per se, assuming a status like that of fiction—"as if Coyote has now entered *our* kind of reality."

The second essay—besides offering a translation of the Indian story recently most discussed and interpreted by literary critics, "Seal and Her Younger Brother Dwelt There"—illustrates contemporary developments crucial to the recognition of Indian artistic narrative. Leading pioneers in this work have been Dell Hymes and Dennis Tedlock, who have both displayed the advantages of transcribing Indian stories not in traditional prose paragraphs (like the free versions cited in this introduction) but by transcriptions reflecting graphically the rhetorical organization that determines the effects of the original tellings.

Hymes, who has worked principally with older published texts, argues that in the original languages one can discover patterns of vocabulary, word formation, syntax, and dramatic parallelism that are the equivalent of Western European literary structures of rhyme, recurrent rhythm, and measured verse. Tedlock, equally vigorous in insisting on the artistry of Indian stories but working with recorded contemporary tellings of traditional myths, has concentrated on identifying the dominant rhetorical forms in the actualities of oral performance. He has devised a transcription system, rather like a musical score, which enables the reader to recognize the significant pauses in a recital and appreciate more fully the meaning of shifts in volume, speed, and tone of voice during a recital. In "Narrative Form as a 'Grammar' of Experience," Hymes beautifully displays their convergent aims and divergent but complementary methods by presenting his own and Tedlock's versions of the Zuni story "Coyote and Junco"; moreover, Tedlock's newest retranslation of the same story, prepared for this edition, follows Hymes's essay.

These two scholars have revolutionized appreciation of traditional Native American storytelling by making it impossible for anyone studying Indian myths today to ignore their artistic dimensions. Like all real revolutions, of course, Hymes's and Tedlock's work has raised a host of profounder questions and has made us perceive the inevitable incompleteness of their discoveries.[8]

Tedlock's insight into the significance of silences in storytelling results in a transcribed "score" of a particular performance, which will probably differ from that of another teller of the same story or even another performance by the same teller. That is the nature of oral performance: every retelling of a story is different from all others, just as each performance of the same piece of music by different violinists, or by the same violinist at different times, is distinct. On the other side, some scholars object that Hymes's elaborate reconstructions of "measured verse" can result in reducing dynamic oral artistry to mechanical renderings (whose structure may be imposed by the translator's interpretation). But those complaints cannot obscure the fundamental value of his many demonstrations that highly wrought formal patterns are often essential to Indian myths. Again and again Hymes has shown that Indian stories mean more to us when we learn how to recognize their formal systematizings. The importance of his demonstrations is revealed through Hymes's commentary on how such rhetorical formalism illuminates the process by which all of us learn our native language.

The third piece in this volume develops some of the most significant implications of Tedlock's transcription method. In his dramatization, or enactment, of how the Zuni beginning happens, Tedlock demonstrates that a Zuni storyteller is necessarily also an interpreter. A Zuni story *continues* to exist vitally because each reciter is simultaneously a reviser. This dialectic of role reflects dialectics in the story, such as the coexistence of the mutually exclusive periods of four years and four days. As impressive is the dialectical definition of the protagonist twins named, by reference to each other, "the Ahayuuta's elder brother" and "the Ahayuuta's younger brother." As Tedlock puts it, "what is called Ahayuuta is between them." Then, too, although they mark the beginning, they always already have a grandmother—named "Ahayuuta's grandmother" or, in Tedlock's words, "Grandmother of difference." Tedlock thus reveals that Zuni oral text and reinterpretation are realized in a continuousness of discourse for which only the most sophisticated of critical procedures (extending and refining approaches developed by, for example, Jacques Derrida, Paul Ricoeur, and Mikhail Bakhtin) will finally be adequate. To illustrate further the interplay of difference-in-continuity that Tedlock displays, I have appended to his essay a very different telling of the Zuni beginning, one recorded by Ruth Bunzel many years ago.

Other forms of verbal artistry that we in our print-dominated culture are likely to misconceive and undervalue are the focus of the next essay. The main subject is a Trickster story, a tale about "Coyote," a being who is simultaneously ridiculous and culturally empowering, a foolish butt of jokes and a self-injuring buffoon who nonetheless releases the profoundest potencies of a community even while making people laugh at his misadventures.[9] The Native American novelist Gerald Vizenor suggests that the Trickster is a communal liberator and healer who comes into being only through oral discourse.[10] In "Poetic Retranslation and the 'Pretty Languages' of Yellowman," Barre Toelken and Tacheeni Scott demonstrate exactly how an audience participates in the social transaction of a Trickster storytelling so as to assure that the deepest principles of Navajo culture are sustained through communal enjoyment of an entertaining narrative.

By posing to this story's teller the paradoxes created by the Trickster, Toelken helps us to understand why this figure can be so baffling to us yet so dynamically central to Indian cultures.

> Why, then, if Coyote is such an important mythic character (whose name must not even be mentioned in the summer months) does Yellowman tell such funny stories about him? Yellowman's answer: "They are not funny stories." Why does everyone laugh, then? "They are laughing at the way Ma'i does things, and at the way the story is told. Many things about the story are funny, but the story is not funny." Why tell the stories? "If my children hear the stories, they will grow up to be good people; if they don't hear them, they will turn out to be bad." Why tell them to adults? "Through the stories everything is made possible."

Inadvertently illustrating what happens when stories are retold, in reanalyzing and retranslating his earlier study of this Navajo Coyote tale, Toelken and Scott discovered that the story's " 'meaning' is no more *in* the texture than it is *in* the structure," because "structure and texture unite to provide an excitement of meaning which already exists elsewhere, in the shared ideas and customs of people raised in an intensely traditional society." Coyote stories "touch off a Navajo's deeper accumulated sense of reality." The "depth" of this reality Toelken fully measured only some years after writing these words, when he was told by revered Navajo medicine men why such stories were so religiously important: "The stories about Coyote are themselves considered so powerful, their recitation in winter so deeply connected to the normal powers of natural cycles, their episodes so reminiscent of central myths . . . that elliptical reference to them in a ritual can . . . summon forth the power of the entire tale and apply it to the healing process . . . to reestablish reality and order." [11] One elderly Navajo healer-singer even suggested to Toelken that his continued inquiry into the religious ramifications of the story he had been studying for thirty years could be "spiritually" damaging to him, a warning that Toelken takes seriously. He does so because the caution confirms, more profoundly than he ever dreamed, his original intuition: even an amusing tale, because its telling and reception activate the most central and vital features of the Navajo system of relationships, radiates enormous sociocultural power the strength of which neither our ethnology nor our criticism has yet succeeded in measuring.

The final and most recently written essay in this collection further concentrates critical attention on mythic content rather than form. Linda Ainsworth analyzes a Wintu myth that makes use of the widespread theme of the "rolling head" cannibal and a more localized pattern of stories of incest. She displays how the mythic imagination works *through* such established cultural structures to evoke in tellers and listeners a shared awareness of the psychic and social pressures that those structures have been constituted to control.

Ainsworth's critique exemplifies a promising line of recent criticism that does not "explain" myths in terms of "universals" but, instead, seeks an understanding of the process of mythic imagining as means for testing and interrogating the necessities from which particular cultural formations arise. This is criticism founded on a supposition that only by understanding the imaginative self-awareness of oral cultures can we—given our secularized, print-dominated perspective—hope to grasp what truly constitutes mythic creations and revisions, and the full range of their psychological and communal functions for tribal peoples. Ainsworth's study shows, for example, how frequently Indian myths focus questions about established social structures by representing problematic gender relations.[12] This procedure, still too little investigated, more often than not centers on themes related to hunting practices, which were almost exclusively a male province.

As a contrastive illustration to suggest this broader value of Ainsworth's approach, I have appended to her essay a Hopi tale, first recorded a century ago but still told by Pueblo people. Even a reader unfamiliar with Pueblo cultures can perceive that the story "plays" with the unexpressed implications in a "childish" game. It "plays dangerously" in order to explore the social and psychological relationships that bind into unity the dynamic (and hence tension-fraught) arbitrary cultural division of gender functions. These are, of course, elaborated from physiological distinctions between the sexes, primary signs of human beings' linkage to their natural environment. The English pun on "game" which this story inevitably evokes for us seems not linguistically paralleled in Hopi, but threateningly problematic sexual connections between adolescent game-playing and adult hunting-for-survival are made dramatically vivid by a story of powers of concealing and discovering, played out among the squash and corn fields that are the agricultural basis of Hopi civilization.

Notes

1. Since the early 1970s there has been a remarkable outpouring of fiction and poetry by a wide variety of Native Americans, among whom one might mention the novelists Louise Erdrich, N. Scott Momaday, Leslie Marmon Silko, Gerald Vizenor, and James Welch and the poets Joy Harjo, Simon Ortiz, Wendy Rose, and Ray A. Youngbear.

2. Alan Dundes, "Texture, Text, and Context," *Southern Folklore Quarterly* 28, no. 4 (1964): 255–56.

3. Text and translation of "The Man Eater" are from Earle Pliny Goddard, *Kato Texts,* University of California Publications in American Archaeology and Ethnology, vol. 5, no. 3 (Berkeley: University of California Press, 1907–10), pp. 179–80, 235–36. Goddard's description and analysis of the Kato language are in volume 11 (1912) of the same series. I have made the following changes in Goddard's orthography of the Kato text: *a* as in *father* = *aa; i* as in *pique* = *ee; u* as in *rule* = *oo;* his *q* = *k;* his *c* for *sh* as in *shall* = *sh;* his *j* as in *azure* = *zh;* his *g* as in German *Tag* = *gh;* his *dj* as *j* in *juice* = *j;* his *tc* and *tc'* = *ch* and *chh,* the added *h* for strong aspiration. An apostrophe indicates glottalizing of preceding sound.

4. "The Fawn, the Wolves, and the Terrapin" appears in John R. Swanton, *Myths and Tales of Southeastern Indians,* Bureau of American Ethnology Bulletin 88 (Washington DC: GPO, 1929), pp. 38–40. I have substituted "sieve" for the regional "riddle." The original collector, W. O. Tuggle, specified that the teller was a woman, and there may be an element of ridicule of masculinity in the story.

5. See Karl Kroeber, *Retelling/Rereading: The Fate of Storytelling in Modern Times* (New Brunswick NJ: Rutgers University Press, 1992), for an extended study of principles of storytelling, using several Native American tales for illustration.

6. Text and translation from Archie Phinney, *Nez Percé Texts,* Columbia University Contributions to Anthropology 25 (New York: Columbia University Press, 1934), pp. 173–76. For details on Phinney's collection, see the following essay by Jarold Ramsey. I reproduce Phinney's orthography of the Nez Percé except for substituting *aa, ee,* and *oo* for the vowels *a, i,* and *u,* as in the Kato text above. The apostrophe indicates glottalizing of the previous sound, and the accent indicates stress, which Phinney identifies (p. xi) as crucial to the rhythm of the telling.

7. See, for example, Herbert Joseph Spinden, *The Nez Percé Indians,* Memoirs of the American Anthropological Association, vol. 2, pt. 3 (N.p., 1908); for a more general discussion of the Indian religious practice, consult a later essay in Ruth Benedict, *The Concept of the Guardian Spirit in North America,* Memoirs of the American Anthropological Association 29 (N.p., 1923).

8. Anthony Mattina, "North American Indian Mythography: Editing Texts for the Printed Page," in *Recovering the Word,* ed. Brian Swann and Arnold Krupat (Berkeley: University

of California Press, 1987), pp. 129–50, raises significant questions about the implications of both Hymes's and Tedlock's innovations.

9. "Coyote" is the best known of the Native American Tricksters, although there are many stories about Raven, Fox, Rabbit, Spider, and various others. In all cases, however, the Trickster is interchangeably human (as in "Coyote and the Shadow People") and animal (as in Yellowman's tale). In Tedlock's terminology, Trickster is "betweenness," a verbal embodiment that simultaneously links and distinguishes nature and culture. Hence his bewildering transformativeness: he sometimes in a single utterance changes from animal to human form and back to animal, and from contemptible buffoon to creator of culture.

10. Gerald Vizenor, "*Trickster Discourse*: Comic Holotropes and Language Games," in *Narrative Chance: Postmodern Discourse on Native American Indian Literatures,* ed. Gerald Vizenor (Albuquerque: University of New Mexico Press, 1989), pp. 187–211.

11. Barre Toelken, "Life and Death in Navajo Coyote Tales," in Swann and Krupat, *Recovering the Word,* p. 390.

12. The Wintu myth Ainsworth analyzes brilliantly dramatizes what physicians now identify as anorexia nervosa, an "illness" of the psychodynamics of a family. As Paula Marantz Cohen, who has studied the relation of this disease to nineteenth-century British fiction, describes the syndrome, "the sick daughter carries the symptoms for the family as a whole, which is generally fraught with multiple covert tensions. The anoretic localizes what would otherwise be a family trauma in the form of her symptoms. . . . The daughter is logically the most prone to occupy the symptomatic role since she is stereotypically conditioned, by reason of age and sex, to be the most accommodating to others' needs." *The Daughter's Dilemma: Family Process and the Nineteenth-Century Domestic Novel* (Ann Arbor: University of Michigan Press, 1991), p. 24.

From "Mythic" to "Fictive"
in a Nez Percé Orpheus Myth

JAROLD RAMSEY

The Orphic story, of a hero's unsuccessful quest to bring back a loved one from the Land of the Dead, is apparently universal among American Indian tribes.[1] In its permutations, the story has a powerful intrinsic appeal that transcends cultural barriers, speaking to us all as mortal humans; and when looked at as oral literature, many of the Indian Orpheus stories reveal, even at the double remove of transcription into print and translation, a striking degree of narrative artistry, as if their anonymous creators were conscious of rising to the occasion of a great theme.

Of such myths, surely one of the most compelling is the Nez Percé "Coyote and the Shadow People," recorded and translated by Archie Phinney in Lapwai, Idaho, in 1929. Now, Phinney's texts are of special value in the study of traditional Western Indian literature because they were collected and edited under nearly perfect conditions. Phinney was a Nez Percé himself, educated at Columbia University and trained in ethnography and linguistics by Franz Boas; and when he returned to the Lapwai Reservation he took as his sole informant his own mother, "Wayilatpu," a gifted storyteller who spoke no English and whose knowledge of her repertory, Phinney tells us, extended back three generations and therefore "beyond the time when the influences of new intertribal contacts and of wholesale myth-trading at nonreservation Indian schools became apparent in Nez Percé mythology."[2]

In terms of classical Boasian scholarship, then, it would be hard to improve upon Phinney's circumstances—they are probably unique among Far Western Indians—and it is clear from his textual work that he brought to it an unusual combination of editorial rigor and literary sensitivity. His translations aim at the more-than-literal re-creation in English of stylistic features in the original narratives; there is a kind of *elegance* to them, which, to be sure, now and then does strike a somewhat stilted Latinate note but which, overall, seems appropriate to stories as rich as these. One of Phinney's great virtues, I think, is his constant awareness of what can be lost in transforming the drama of oral narrative into print—lines on a page. As he complained in a letter to Boas, "A sad thing in recording these animal stories is the loss of spirit—the fascination furnished by the peculiar Indian vocal tradition for humor. Indians are better story-tellers than whites. When I read my story mechanically I find only the cold corpse." [3]

The final sentence of Phinney's introduction to his collection is an eloquent plea—one worth heeding now as we set out to examine just one of his people's stories—against reading the stories mechanically, out of context, and for, instead, opening the imagination to them as a mythology. He says, "Any substantial appreciation of these tales must come not from the simple elements of drama unfolded but from vivid feeling within oneself, feeling as a moving current all the figures and the relationships that belong to the whole mythbody." [4]

Now for the story, "Coyote and the Shadow People."

Coyote and his wife were dwelling there. His wife became ill. She died. Then Coyote became very, very lonely. He did nothing but weep for his wife.

There the death spirit came to him and said, "Coyote, do you pine for your wife?" — "Yes, friend, I long for her . . ." replied Coyote. "I could take you to the place where your wife has gone, but, I tell you, you must do everything just exactly as I say; not once are you to disregard my commands and do something else." — "Yes," replied Coyote, "yes, friend, and what else could I do? I will do everything you say." Then the ghost told him, "Yes. Now let us go." Coyote added, "Yes, let it be so that we are going."

They went. There he said to Coyote again, "You must do whatever I say. Do not disobey." — "Yes, yes, friend. I have been pining so deeply, and why should I not heed you?" Coyote could not see the spirit clearly. He appeared to be only a shadow. They started and went along over a plain. "Oh, there are many horses; it looks like a round-up," exclaimed the ghost. "Yes," replied Coyote, though he really saw none, "yes, there are many horses."

They had arrived now near the place of the dead. The ghost knew that Coyote could see nothing but he said, "Oh look, such quantities of service berries! Let us pick some to eat. Now when you see me reach up you too will reach up and when I bend the limb down you too will pull your hands down." — "Yes," Coyote said to him, "so be it, thus I will do." The ghost reached up and bent the branch down and Coyote did the same. Although he could see no berries he imitated the ghost in putting his hand to and from his mouth in the manner of eating. Thus they picked and ate berries. Coyote watched him carefully and imitated every action. When the ghost would put his hand into his mouth Coyote would do the same. "Such good service berries these are," commented the ghost. "Yes, friend, it is good that we have found them," agreed Coyote. "Now let us go." And they went on.

"We are about to arrive," the ghost told him. "There is a long, very, very long lodge. Your wife is in there somewhere. Just wait and let me ask someone." In a little while the ghost returned and said to Coyote, "Yes, they have told me where your wife is. We are coming to a door through which we will enter. You will do in every way exactly what you see me do. I will take hold of the door flap, raise it up, and bending low, will enter. Then you too will take hold of the door flap and do the same." They proceeded now in this manner to enter.

It happened that Coyote's wife was sitting right near the entrance. The ghost said to Coyote, "Sit here beside your wife." They both sat. The ghost added, "Your wife is now going to prepare food for us." Coyote could see nothing, except that he was sitting there on an open prairie where nothing was in sight; yet he could feel the presence of the shadow. "Now she has prepared our food. Let us eat." The ghost reached down and then brought his hand to his mouth. Coyote could see nothing but the prairie dust. They ate. Coyote imitated all the movements of his companion. When they had finished and the woman had apparently put the food away, the ghost said to Coyote, "You stay here. I must go around to see some people."

He went out but returned soon. "Here we have conditions different from those you have in the land of the living. When it gets dark here it has dawned in your land and when it dawns for us it is growing dark for you." And now it began to grow dark and Coyote seemed to hear people whispering, talking in faint tones, all around him. Then darkness set in. Oh, Coyote saw many fires in a long-house. He saw that he was in a very, very large lodge and there were many fires burning. He saw the various people. They seemed to have shadow-like forms but he was able to recognize different persons. He saw his wife sitting by his side.

He was overjoyed, and he joyfully greeted all his old friends who had died long ago. How happy he was! He would march down the aisles between the fires, going here and there, and talk with the people. He did this throughout the night. Now he could see the doorway through which he and his friend had entered. At last it began to dawn and his friend came to him and said, "Coyote, our night is falling and in a little while you will not see us. But you must stay right here. Do not go anywhere at all. Stay right here and then in the evening you will see all these people again." — "Yes, friend. Where could I possibly go? I will spend the day here."

The dawn came and Coyote found himself alone sitting there in the middle of a prairie. He spent the day there, just dying from the heat, parching from the heat, thirsting from the heat. Coyote stayed here several days. He would suffer through the day, but always at night he would make merry in the great lodge.

One day his ghost friend came to him and said, "Tomorrow you will go home. You will take your wife with you." — "Yes, friend, but I like it here so much, I am having a good time and I should like to remain here." — "Yes," the ghost replied; "nevertheless you will go tomorrow, and you must guard against your inclination to do foolish things. Do not yield to any queer notions. I will advise you now what you are to do. There are five mountains. You will travel for five days. Your wife will be with you but you must never, never touch her. Do not let any strange impulses possess you. You may talk to her but never touch her. Only after you have crossed and descended from the fifth mountain you may do whatever you like." — "Yes, friend," replied Coyote.

When dawn came again Coyote and his wife started. At first it seemed to him as if he were going alone, yet he was dimly aware of his wife's presence as she walked along behind. They crossed one mountain, and, now, Coyote could feel more definitely the presence of his wife; like a shadow she seemed. They went on and crossed the second mountain. They camped at night at the foot of each mountain. They had a little conical lodge which they would set up each time. Coyote's wife would sit on one side of the fire and he on the other. Her form appeared clearer and clearer.

The death spirit, who had sent them, now began to count the days and to figure the distance Coyote and his wife had covered. "I hope that he will do everything right and take his wife through to the world beyond," he kept saying to himself.

Here Coyote and his wife were spending their last night, their fourth camping, and on the morrow she would again assume fully the character of a living person. They were camping for the last time and Coyote could see her very clearly as if she were a real person who sat opposite him. He could see her face and body very clearly, but only looked and dared not touch her.

But suddenly a joyous impulse seized him; the joy of having his wife again overwhelmed him. He jumped to his feet and rushed over to embrace her. His wife cried out, "Stop! Stop! Coyote! Do not touch me. Stop!" Her warning had no effect. Coyote rushed over to his wife and just as he touched her body she vanished. She disappeared— returned to the shadow-land.

When the death spirit learned of Coyote's folly he became deeply angry. "You inveterate doer of this kind of thing! I told you not to do anything foolish. You, Coyote, were about to establish the practice of returning from death. Only a short time away the human race is coming, but you have spoiled everything and established for them death as it is."

Here Coyote wept and wept. He decided, "Tomorrow I shall return to see them again." He started back the following morning and as he went along he began to recognize the places where he and his spirit friend had passed before. He found the place where the ghost had seen the herd of horses, and now he began to do the same things they had done on their way to the shadow-land. "Oh, look at the horses; it looks like a round-up." He went on until he came to the place where the ghost had found the service berries. "Oh, such choice service berries! Let us pick and eat some." He went through the motions of picking and eating berries.

He went on and finally came to the place where the lodge had stood. He said to himself, "Now when I take hold of the door flap and raise it up you must do the same." Coyote remembered all the little things his friend had done. He saw the spot where he had sat before. He went there, sat down, and said, "Now, your wife has brought us food. Let us eat." He went through the motions of eating again. Darkness fell, and now Coyote listened for the voices, and he looked all around, he looked here and there, but nothing appeared. Coyote sat there in the middle of the prairie. He sat there all night but the lodge didn't appear again nor did the ghost ever return to him.[5]

More than most of the other narratives in *Nez Percé Texts,* "Coyote and the Shadow People" is intelligible without extensive ethnographic commentary, but it is helpful to know the hero, Coyote, *itsayáya,* is usually a wily but reckless, self-seeking Trickster and adventurer in Nez Percé myths, much given to opportunistic deceptions (often for sex) that usually backfire outrageously. His classical mythic name in this role, according to Phinney, is *nasáwaylu.*[6] But like the Trickster in other Western Indian mythologies, Coyote is also the Nez Percé "transformer," the Myth Age personage who "travels about" transforming the unfinished world and its inhabitants and setting precedents (for better and for worse) that create reality as the latter-day Indians knew it. So, in this Orphic story, the awesome mythic powers in Coyote's complex role are emphasized, and to some extent he is made to seem capable of living up to these powers, as in his sustained grief for his wife and his persistence in seeking her. But the narrator clearly reminds us of Coyote's reputation as a Trickster, *nasáwaylu,* in the spirit guide's repeated warnings against doing "foolish things" and of course in his denunciation of Coyote near the end.

The mysterious "lodge of shadows" where Coyote finds his wife presumably had its real-life counterpart in the long pole-and-mat structures of the Nez Percés, pitched like tipis side by side with a continuous ridgepole; such a lodge, over one hundred feet long, was erected to house the death feast of the great Nez Percé leader Joseph at Nespelem, Washington, in 1904.[7] Conceptually, the lodge reflects a widespread Western Indian view of the afterlife as a remote condition of the spirit in which the basic circumstances of earthly life are inverted: the night of the living is the daytime of the dead and vice versa; what is tangible to them is intangible to us (and the reverse), and so on. A morally neutral location—there is no alternative destination for the sinful—the Indian spirit place seems to be at best a kind of eschatological afterthought, a "lodge of shadows" indeed, where the surviving spirits exist not unpleasantly but without the raw immediacy and sweetness of mortal life. Early missionaries among the Nez Percés and other Great Plateau tribes were baffled by this conception of the essential goodness of earthly life set off by contrast with images of a shadowy, static afterlife; one of them, the Catholic Father Blanchet, complained that his native subjects "were surprised and provoked when I explained to them the blessedness of heaven; they appeared to like better the sojourn on this earth than to go away to enjoy celestial bliss." [8]

The narrative and dramatic strategies of "Coyote and the Shadow People" are conventional in native terms and typical of Western Indian literature; and yet they seem, as they combine in this story, to achieve an imaginative power that is remarkable. In common with most Orphic stories, Indian and otherwise, the structure is highly symmetrical, details from before Coyote's arrival at the lodge corresponding to those coming afterward—a Journey In, and a Journey Out. Thus, the death of his wife, his mourning, and the initial appearance of the spirit guide are balanced by the final loss of his wife, his second mourning, and the final appearance of the spirit guide; his initial ritualized journey to the "lodge of shadows" is paralleled by the ritual stages of his journey back with his wife. In this symmetrical structure, only two main events are singular, set off by themselves—his joyful reunion with his dead wife, and his solitary second journey to the lodge—and the special significance of their being isolated as single actions we will see in a moment.

Of all the narrative strategies employed in Indian myth, *foreshadowing* appears most frequently and with the widest latitude of effects. This has everything to do, of course, with the fact that the stories were well known in outline to tribal audiences; with the outcome of a given story foreknown, the recitalist had a built-in condition of dramatic irony to exploit.[9] In the case of a story like "Coyote and the Shadow People," the ironic foreshadowing carries over beyond what only a Nez Percé listener would have recognized: we *all* know, after all, with varying degrees of conviction, that death is irrevocable and final. Thus in a sense everything Coyote does in his quest foreshadows his failure, both for himself and his wife and for the great precedent of returning from death that he (as the death spirit's unknowing instrument) might establish. And yet, true to its genre (and to human nature), the story does set our unresigned human imaginations against our mortal knowledge of death's finality. We lend Coyote our dreams.

Specific prefigurements occur at every turn. There is the spirit guide's initial stern demand that Coyote—of all people, the Nez Percé Trickster!—must follow his instructions exactly, unquestioningly. The strange ritual en route involving invisible horses, a tent flap, and a meal are clearly *tests* of Coyote's imagination and will; he is rewarded for his unaccustomed self-control by seeing his wife and dead associates, but in the daytime, ominously, he loses all sight of them and must "suffer through the day," "sitting there in the middle of a prairie" — the latter phrase a verbatim anticipation of the story's final narrative line. His complacent wish to remain in the lodge instead of returning home with his wife evidently contradicts the purposes of the spirit guide, both for Coyote and his wife and for the human race to come, and it too foreshadows the end. So does the spirit guide's unexplained injunction against touching his wife on the return trip: like all such taboos, it implies its own eventual tragic violation.

As for their journey back, the landscape through which Coyote and his wife travel is ritualized and programmatic, the five mountains serving as checkpoints for Coyote's tense progress; the brief appearance of the spirit guide at this point in the story, worrying about his protégé, notably heightens the tension. (Such intrusions are in fact uncommon in Western Indian narratives.) The fact that Coyote's wife grows day by day more tangible and real to him, of course, dramatizes the progressive heroic success of his quest to him—at the same time that it brings him, all too human, closer and closer to the forbidden but irresistible embrace, in a kind of vectoring of encouragement and temptation.

The climax, by the time it comes, is wholly foreshadowed; as usual, according to the *dramatic* premises of Indian narrative, its enactment is stark, tacit, "dramatic." We must imagine for ourselves the emotional reality evoked so economically by Coyote's impulsive gesture and his wife's cry—her one speech in the story.[10] That Coyote's loss of his wife, and indeed his unknowing forfeiture of the Orphic dream, should hinge on his inability to resist *touching* her rather than looking back at her, as in the Greek prototypes and many Indian versions, seems to me beautifully calculated to express the tragic paradox in Coyote's situation. He has been *seeing* his dead wife for some time, but now that she appears to be fully tangible, seeing is not enough. To return to life again is to touch and be touched, ultimately in a sexual sense; Coyote would not "foolishly" violate the taboo and lose her if he did not love and desire her so much. To put the paradox another way, in terms of literary effect: if he *could* "take the long view" and restrain himself, the reality of his feelings for his wife would surely be suspect. The story asks its unblinking mythic question of us, Coyote's mortal inheritors: *Would we be able to do otherwise?* Well, at the level on which the story speaks to us as good citizens, obeyers of laws and keepers of taboos, I suppose we do answer, "Oh yes, we'd better do otherwise!" But to answer, on the heart's own level, "No, probably not," as I think we must, is to feel the peculiar mood of this myth—chastened, instructed, consoled. People die, we are reminded, and we cannot bring them back because they—and we—are in the nature of things imperfect, shortsighted, alive chiefly in the present moment; that is to say, we are mortal. The "truth" of all mythology is, finally, tautological.

Before taking up the story's final episode, I want to digress briefly on some parallels to this moment of climax and reversal in other native Orpheus stories from the Oregon country, to at least point toward the imaginative diversity and psychological subtlety inherent in this kind of narrative. In the Wasco and Wishram Chinookan versions, as told along the Columbia River, Coyote and Eagle (a wise headman) both lose their wives; after Eagle leads them on a highly complicated raid on the Lodge of Spirits and they are headed home again with a box containing the spirits of their wives and everyone else who has died, as well as samples of deciduous plants, Coyote begins to hear his wife's voice from within the box. Unable to wait until they reach home—there is no taboo as such—Coyote tricks Eagle into letting him carry the box and seizes the first opportunity to unfasten the lid—whereupon all the spirits, including his wife, fly off in a great swarm, leaving only the plant samples in the box. Eagle denounces Coyote for his impatience, explaining that if they had gotten the box home intact, all people, as well as the trees and grasses, would have died only for a season and then returned to life.[11]

In Melville Jacobs's great collection of Clackamas Chinook stories, there is an Orphic variant titled "Badger and Coyote Were Neighbors."[12] When Coyote's five children are killed trying to steal a wonderful ball from another village (as their ambitious and greedy father has urged them to do), he first attempts suicide by fire, water, and knife; then, in the following spring, he undertakes to collect his children's bones and carry them home in such a magical way that they will be reanimated. Day by day he carries them homeward in his basket, very, very carefully; so slowly and deliberately does he move that on the fourth night he can look back and see his previous night's campfire. By now he can hear his children talking to one another. On the fifth and final day, however, an insect of some sort, "maybe a centipede," appears in Coyote's path and taunts him by sniffing the air and declaring that "Coyote is carrying dead persons along!" At first Coyote controls himself, but at last he loses his temper and chases after the insect—with the result that his nearly revived children are jostled and they die again, and with them all hope of bringing loved ones back, "just so," from death. It is left for Coyote, sadder and wiser, to invent the customs of mourning, whereby a mourner's grief will be limited in deference to the welfare of the tribe.

A few comparisons. In all three stories Coyote takes his fatal hasty step in ignorance of the great human precedent he is throwing away: given his chronic self-centeredness and preoccupation with the moment, perhaps the point is being made that such grave knowledge would be irrelevant to him anyway, as a guide to action. He is inconstant and fallible—like us. The Wishram and Clackamas stories seem to have a wider etiological scope than the Nez Percé in that they couple the lost human precedent of returning from death with the achieved precedent of seasonal revivals among plants, as in the Persephone myth; the Nez Percé Coyote is denied even that Wordsworthian consolation. As for the moment of truth itself, you can take your pick from three wonderfully vivid dramatizations, each having its own fix on human frailty and desire: the Wishram Coyote singling his wife's voice out of all the buzzing in the spirit box, "like a great swarm of flies"; or the marvelous psychological projection of the Clackamas Coyote's internal doubts and impatience on finding a mocking insect in his path; or, again, the stark detail of the Nez Percé Coyote's *seeing* his wife's living body again, across the fire. Do we really want to call this kind of art "primitive"?

Now to carry on with the structure of the Nez Percé story. Before, we noticed that two of its events are structurally singular and unbalanced—Coyote's re-union with his wife, and his second quest for her, by himself. The reunion stands alone, of course, because the return to life and home of which it is to be an initial stage, is doomed. As for Coyote's second quest, begun after the final meaning of his Orphic failure has been emphatically spelled out to him, so far as I know it is unique in North American native literature. In this sur-prising final episode the narrative seems to move beyond the modus and logic of myth per se, assuming a status more like that of fiction—as if Coyote has now entered *our* kind of reality.

At the end of many Indian Orpheus stories, the failed quester *wants* to go back after his lost loved one but will not or cannot oppose the precedent he has just established. In Phinney's other Orpheus story, for example, after Coyote has "looked back" and thus lost his chance to carry his daughter all the way back from death, he pleads, "Let me follow you back and I will bring you again"; but the offer is refused, and after a little weeping he wanders off.[13] But here, on some level of consciousness at least, Coyote actually does set out again, as if moving beyond the finalized terms of his own myth as explained to him by the spirit guide. Now it is possible that this episode would have struck Nez

Percé listeners as a kind of ironic analogue to the solitary and highly ritualized visionary quests on which all native religions in the Far West were founded— Coyote, having had genuine commerce with the spirit world and having violated its terms, can now only go through the motions, as if in a dream. Indeed, it may be that behind all the weird journeys and heroic ordeals in Nez Percé and other Western repertoires there stands, ultimately, the cultural archetype of the spirit quest.[14]

But this is extracurricular speculation, and I think a more helpful literary parallel to the episode of Coyote's attempted return can be found in myths, from a variety of tribes, which dramatize the origin of death itself. Typically, a Myth Age person decrees that according to some abstract philanthropical principle—the danger of overcrowding and famine, for example—people will have to die. Then the decreer in fact suffers the first mortal loss (often it is a child who dies) and, humanlike, pleads unavailingly with the Creator for a repeal or postponement of the new law. In the Blackfoot "Old Man" cycle, for instance, First Woman opts for universal human mortality for a compelling but highly abstract reason: "so people will be sorry for one another." [15] But when her son dies soon afterward, she rejects this wisdom and begs "Old Man," unsuccessfully, to change the Way. Like Coyote in his second return, First Woman appears to move beyond her mythic situation per se into the common tragic experience of mortality; she and Coyote both actively "suffer," as if in a fictive work, their own myths, as we do in real life who follow them.[16]

Where before, Coyote is, as we say, all too human in wanting so ardently to touch his wife for a moment that he loses her forever, so here in this post-Orphic sequel he is shown to be poignantly, definitively human in his confidence that his own unaided imagination and desire, supplemented by a little ceremonial knowledge, will suffice to carry him back to the lodge of the shadow people and his wife, despite the mythic precedent he has just set. His actions in retracing his steps and playing both himself and the spirit guide "just so" are at once heroic and ridiculous; here he becomes most fully integrated as himself, Coyote *itsayáya* and *nasáwaylu*. The end of his quest, with Coyote sitting alone "there in the middle of the prairie," has an affective resonance and finality beyond any other Orpheus story I know.

Wayilatpu's Nez Percé narrative gives us Coyote as an image—of human loss—mythically speaking, the first in a long unbroken line of unresigned mourners who again and again wake up from their Orphic dreams into what Yeats called "the desolation of reality." [17] But it is a desolation for which, through the story, we have words and a human image.

Notes

1. A version of this essay was read at the 1976 meeting of the Rocky Mountain Modern Language Association, in Santa Fe, New Mexico, October 1976. The essay originally appeared in *Western American Literature* 13, no. 2 (1978). On the Orpheus theme see Äke Hultkrantz's very full study, *The North American Indian Orpheus Tradition,* Ethnological Museum of Sweden Monograph Series 2 (Stockholm, 1957); oddly enough, Hultkrantz ignores "Coyote and the Shadow People," the text discussed here. Also see Anne Gayton, "The Orpheus Myth in North America," *Journal of American Folklore* 48, no. 2 (1935): 263–93. Gayton's study apparently came out too early for her to consider Phinney's collection.

2. Archie Phinney, *Nez Percé Texts,* Columbia University Contributions to Anthropology 25 (New York: Columbia University Press, 1934), p. vii.

3. Phinney to Boas, 20 November 1929, MS letter in the collection of the American Philosophical Society Library, Philadelphia, printed here with the permission of the Society.

4. Phinney, *Nez Percé Texts,* p. ix.

5. Phinney, *Nez Percé Texts,* pp. 282–85. Phinney presents the story as a "second version" of another Orpheus story, "Coyote the Interloper" (pp. 268–81), but in fact the two are radically different. For reasons unknown to me Phinney does not give the Nez Percé language text for "Coyote and the Shadow People," as he does for the rest of his stories. The English text is reprinted, with notes, in my anthology *Coyote Was Going There: Indian Literature of the Oregon Country* (Seattle: University of Washington Press, 1977).

6. In Phinney's collection, for example, see "Coyote Causes His Son to Be Lost," "Bat and Coyote," and "Bears and Coyote," in which (p. 480) a Bear says to Coyote, "Vile you are, Coyote" (*nasáwaylu*).

7. For an account of the event, and photographs of the lodge, see Edward S. Curtis, *The North American Indian* (Norwood MA: Plimpton, 1911), 8:40. The appearance of the lodge and the reference to the "conical lodge" (tipi) that Coyote and his wife use en route home, in connection with the references to horses and a roundup, suggest that the story as we have it dates from no earlier than the middle of the eighteenth century, after the appearance of horses and horseback encounters with Plains culture.

8. Father Blanchet in *Notices and Voyages of the Famous Quebec Mission to the Pacific Northwest,* ed. and trans. Carl Landerholm (Portland OR: Champoey, 1956), p. 68.

9. I discuss the use and effects of foreshadowing in "The Wife Who Goes Out like a Man, Comes Back as a Hero," *PMLA* 92, no. 1 (1977): 9–18.

10. It is a measure of this story's pervasive seriousness that, whereas in other Phinney texts Coyote is variously—and comically—married to wives identified as Mouse (evidently his favorite), "Lady Bullfrog," White Swan, and "flying people," here the wife has no animal or typological identity; she is only "Coyote's wife" and is recognized only by him and by the spirit guide.

11. The Wishram story is in Curtis, *The North American Indian,* 8:127–29; it follows these notes, as does the story cited in note 12. Another Wishram version is in Edward Sapir, *Wishram Texts,* Publications of the American Ethnological Society 2 (Leyden NJ: E. J. Brill, 1909), pp. 107–17; the same collection contains a Wasco version transcribed by Jeremiah Curtin (pp. 127–29).

12. Text and commentary are given in Melville Jacobs's pioneering study, *The Content and Style of an Oral Literature: Clackamas Chinook Texts,* Viking Fund Publications in Anthropology 26 (Chicago: University of Chicago Press, 1959), pp. 27–36.

13. Phinney, *Nez Percé Texts,* p. 282.

14. For ethnographic commentary see Herbert Spinden, *The Nez Percé Indians,* Memoirs of the American Anthropological Association, vol. 2, pt. 3 (N.p., 1908); and Curtis, *The North American Indian,* 8:52–76.

15. George Bird Grinnell, *Blackfoot Lodge Tales* (1892; rpt. Lincoln: University of Nebraska Press, 1962), p. 139. For a view of Tricksters as creators of death in some Indian myths, see M. L. Ricketts, "The North American Indian Trickster," *History of Religions* 5 (1966): 327–50.

16. In "Serial Order in Nez Percé Myths," *Journal of American Folklore* 84, no. 2 (1971): 104–17, Brian Stross examines "myth initials" and "myth finals"—the opening and closing expressions of the narratives—in relation to other kinds of serial order in them and finds two kinds of myth finals: "Either the audience leaves the scene of action while the actor or actors remain in a state of relative inaction . . . or else the actor or actors leave the scene of action without a corresponding shift of scene by the narrator." In the second form of ending "the audience is transported from the world of myth to the world of reality by means of an explanatory connection between the two" (p. 108). In the case of "Coyote and the Shadow People," Coyote's last episode seems to conclude with Stross's first kind of myth final, and yet in *effect*—our sense of movement from mythic to fictive representation of reality—it seems to correspond to his second kind, albeit without formulaic expression or "explanatory connection." In fact, those elements have already appeared at what would be the conventional ending of the story, before Coyote's last quest, when the death spirit tells him, "Only a short time away the human race is coming, but you have spoiled everything and established for them death as it is."

17. William Butler Yeats, "Meru," *The Collected Poems of William Butler Yeats* (New York: Macmillan, 1950), p. 333. Informant unknown, transcription and translation probably by W. E. Myers.

The Origin of Eternal Death *

Coyote had a wife and two children, and so had Eagle. Both families lived together. Eagle's wife and children died, and a few days later Coyote experienced the same misfortune. As the latter wept, his companion said, "Do not mourn: that will not bring your wife back. Make ready your moccasins, and we will go somewhere." So the two prepared for a long journey, and set out westward.

After four days they were close to the ocean; on one side of a body of water they saw houses. Coyote called across, "Come with a boat!" "Never mind; stop calling," bade Eagle. He produced an elderberry stalk, made a flute, put the end into the water, and whistled. Soon they saw two persons come out of a house, walk to the water's edge, and enter a canoe. Said Eagle, "Do not look at those people when they land." The boat drew near, but a few yards from the shore it stopped, and Eagle told his friend to close his eyes. He then took Coyote by the arm and leaped to the boat. The two persons paddled back, and when they stopped a short distance from the other side Eagle again cautioned Coyote to close his eyes, and then leaped ashore with him.

They went to the village, where there were many houses, but no people were in sight. Everything was still as death. There was a very large underground house, into which they went. In it was found an old woman sitting with her face to the wall, and lying on the floor on the other side of the room was the moon. They sat down near the wall.

"Coyote," whispered Eagle, "watch that woman and see what she does when the sun goes down!" Just before the sun set they heard a voice outside calling, "Get up! Hurry! The sun is going down, and it will soon be night. Hurry, hurry!" Coyote and Eagle still sat in a corner of the chamber watching the old woman. People began to enter, many hundreds of them, men, women, and children. Coyote, as he watched, saw Eagle's wife and two daughters among them, and soon afterward his own family. When the room was filled, Nikshiámchásht, the old woman, cried, "Are all in?" Then she turned about, and from a squatting posture she jumped forward, then again and again, five times in all, until she alighted in a small pit beside the moon. This she raised and swallowed, and at once it was pitch dark. The people wandered about, hither and thither, crowding and jostling, unable to see. About daylight a voice from outside cried, "Nikshiámchásht, all get through!" The old woman then disgorged the moon, and laid it back in its place on the floor; all the people filed out, and the woman, Eagle, and Coyote were once more alone.

"Now, Coyote," said Eagle, "could you do that?" "Yes, I can do that," he said. They

---

*Edward S. Curtis, *The North American Indian* (Norwood MA: Plimpton, 1911), 8:127–29. Informant, unknown; transcription and translation, probably by W. E. Myers.

went out, and Coyote at Eagle's direction made a box of boards, as large as he could carry, and put into it leaves from every kind of tree and blades from every kind of grass. "Well," said Eagle, "if you are sure you remember just how she did this, let us go in and kill her." So they entered the house and killed her, and buried the body. Her dress they took off and put on Coyote, so that he looked just like her, and he sat down in her place. Eagle then told him to practise what he had seen, by turning around and jumping as the old woman had done. So Coyote turned about and jumped five times, but the last leap was a little short, yet he managed to slide into the hole. He put the moon into his mouth, but, try as he would, a thin edge still showed, and he covered it with his hands. Then he laid it back in its place and resumed his seat by the wall, waiting for sunset and the voice of the chief outside.

The day passed, the voice called, and the people entered. Coyote turned about and began to jump. Some thought there was something strange about the manner of jumping, but others said it was really the old woman. When he came to the last jump and slipped into the pit, many cried out that this was not the old woman, but Coyote quickly lifted the moon and put it into his mouth, covering the edge with his hands. When it was completely dark, Eagle placed the box in the doorway. Throughout the long night Coyote retained the moon in his mouth, until he was almost choking, but at last the voice of the chief was heard from the outside, and the dead began to file out. Every one walked into the box, and Eagle quickly threw the cover over and tied it. The sound was like that of a great swarm of flies. "Now, my brother, we are through," said Eagle. Coyote removed the dress and laid it down beside the moon, and Eagle threw the moon into the sky, where it remained. The two entered the canoe with the box, and paddled toward the east.

When they landed, Eagle carried the box. Near the end of the third night Coyote heard somebody talking; there seemed to be many voices. He awakened his companion, and said, "There are many people coming." "Do not worry," said Eagle; "it is all right." The following night Coyote heard the talking again, and, looking about, he discovered that the voices came from the box which Eagle had been carrying. He placed his ear against it, and after a while distinguished the voice of his wife. He smiled, and broke into laughter, but he said nothing to Eagle. At the end of the fifth night and the beginning of their last day of travelling, he said to his friend, "I will carry the box now; you have carried it a long way." "No," replied Eagle, "I will take it; I am strong." "Let me carry it," insisted the other; "suppose we come to where people live, and they should see the chief carrying the load. How would that look?" Still Eagle retained his hold on the box, but as they went along Coyote kept begging, and about noon, wearying of the subject, Eagle gave him the box. So Coyote had the load, and every time he heard the voice of his wife he would laugh. After a while he contrived to fall behind, and when Eagle was out of sight around a hill he began to open the box, in order to release his wife. But no sooner was the cover lifted than it was thrown back violently, and the dead people rushed out into the air with such force that Coyote was thrown to the ground. They quickly disappeared in the west. Eagle saw the cloud of dead people rising in the air, and came hurrying back. He found one man left there, a cripple who had been unable to rise; he threw him into the air, and the dead man floated away swiftly.

"You see what you have done, with your curiosity and haste!" said Eagle. "If we had brought these dead all the way back, people would not die forever, but only for a season, like these plants, whose leaves we have brought. Hereafter trees and grasses will die only in the winter, but in the spring they will be green again. So it would have been with the people." "Let us go back and catch them again," proposed Coyote; but Eagle objected: "They will not go to the same place, and we would not know how to find them; they will be where the moon is, up in the sky."

Badger and Coyote Were Neighbors*

Coyote and his five children lived there (at an undisclosed location), four males, one female. Badger was a neighbor there, he had five children, all males. Each day they (all ten children) would go here and there. They came back in the evening. And the next day they would go again. Now that is the way they were doing. They would go all over, they traveled about.

Now they reached a village, they stayed up above there, they looked down below at it, they saw where they (the villagers) were playing ball. And as they stayed there and watched, the people (of the village beneath) saw them now. They went to the place there where they played ball. Now they (the villagers) played. When they threw the ball it (that ball) was just like the sun. Now they stayed (above) there, they watched them playing. Sometimes it (the ball) would drop close by them. Now they quit (playing). Then they (the ten children who were watching) went back home, they went to their houses.

The next day then they did not go anywhere. All day long they chatted about that ball (and schemed about stealing it). They discussed it. Now their father Badger heard them. He said to his sons, "What is it that you are discussing?" So they told their father. "Yes," they said to him, "we got to a village, and they were playing ball. When the ball went it was just like the sun. We thought that we would go get it." Now then he said to his children, "What do you think (about talking this over with Coyote too)?" So then

*Melville Jacobs, *The Content and Style of an Oral Literature: Clackamas Chinook Myths and Tales,* Viking Fund Publications in Anthropology 26 (Chicago: University of Chicago Press, 1959), pp. 27–29. © 1959 by Wenner-Gren Foundation for Anthropological Research, Inc. Reprinted with permission. Informant, Victoria Howard.

they said to Coyote, "What do you think?" He said, "My children should be the first ones (to run with the ball), if they bring the ball." Badger said, "No. My children should be the first ones to do it (run with the stolen ball)." Coyote said, "No. My children have long bodies, their legs are long. They can run (faster than your children). Your children have short legs." So then he replied to him (to Coyote), "Very well then."

Now the next day they got ready, and they went. They reached there. At that place one of them (the oldest son of Coyote) went immediately to the spot where the ball might drop. He covered (buried) himself at that place (on the playing field). Then another (the next oldest son) buried himself farther on, and another one (the third in age) still farther away. All four (sons of Coyote) covered themselves (with soil on the field). The last one farther on at the end (was) their younger sister. Now the (five) children of Badger merely remained (on the hill above the field), they watched.

Soon afterwards then the people (of that village) came to there, they came to play ball. Now they threw the ball to where it fell close by him (Coyote's oldest son). He seized it. They looked for it, they said (because they knew that), "Coyote's son is hiding it!" He let it go, and they took it, and they played more. Now it dropped close by him there once again. So then he took it, and he ran. The people turned and looked, they saw him running, he was taking the ball. Now they ran in pursuit, they got close to him, he got close to his younger brother (the second in age), he threw the ball to him. He said to him, "We are dying (going to be killed) because of the ball. Give a large chunk of it to our father." (His pursuers now caught up to and killed him.) Then the other (the second) one took it, and he ran too. The people pursued him, he got close to his young brother (Coyote's third son). Now they seized him (the second son), and he threw it to his younger brother. They killed all four of them. Now only their younger sister held the ball, she ran, she ran and ran, she left them quite a distance (behind because she was the fastest runner of them all). She got close to the Badgers. Now as they (the villagers who pursued) seized her she threw the ball to them (to the five Badger children), she said to them, "Give the biggest portion to our father (to Coyote). We have died because of the ball."

The Badgers took the ball. He (the first and oldest Badger child) dropped it when he picked it up. Another (the next to the oldest) took it, he also dropped it when he picked it up. They (the pursuers) got to there, and the people stood there (watching the Badger children fumbling the ball). They said, they told them, "So those are the ones who would be taking away the ball!" They laughed at them (at the seemingly clumsy Badger children). They said, "Let it be a little later before we kill them!" Soon now they (the Badgers) kicked at the ground, and wind blew (and) dust (and) darkness stood there. Dust covered (everything), and the wind blew. Now the Badgers ran, they ran away with the ball. And those people pursued them. They got tired, they got thirsty (from wind and dust), they (the pursuers) turned back to their home.

On the other hand those others (the Badgers) lay down (because of exhaustion) right there when they had gotten close (to their own home). And there they sat (and rested). Now they hallooed, they said to their father, "Badger! we left your children far back there!" Now they hallooed again, they went and told Coyote, "Back yonder we left your children." That is the way they did to them (they first deceived Badger and Coyote). Now Badger went outside, he said to his children, "Now really why did you do like that? You have been teasing and paining him (Coyote)." Then they (the Badger children) went downhill (and entered the village), it was only Badger's children (who returned). They brought the ball with them.

Now Coyote tried in vain to drown himself. He did not die. Then he built a fire, he made a big fire, he leaped into it there. He did not burn, he did not die. He took a rope, he tied it, he tied it on his throat, he pulled himself up, once more he did not die. He took a knife, he cut his throat, (again) he did not die. He did every sort of thing that he intended for killing himself. He gave up. I do not know how many days he was doing like that (trying one or another means of committing suicide). Now he quit it, and he merely wept all the day long. (After a while) he gave that up (too).

Then Badger said to his children, "He has quit (mourning) now. So then cut up the ball for him. Give him half." And they did that for him, they gave him half. He took it, and he went here and there at the place where his children used to play. There he now mashed (into many pieces) that ball, at the place where they used to play. That was where he took it, he mashed it up, the ball was entirely gone (now).

Then they continued to live there, and Coyote was all alone. Now he went to work, he made a loose big pack basket. Then it was getting to be springtime, and when the leaves were coming out, now he got ready, and he went to the place there where they had killed his children. He got to the (grave of the) first one (his oldest son). He picked ferns, he lined his pack basket with them. He got to the place where they had killed the first of his sons, he collected his bones, he put them into it (into the basket), he laid them in it neatly. Then he got more ferns, he picked the leaves, he covered (the bones of) his son. Now he went a little farther, and he again got to bones (of his second son). Then he also put them into it (into the basket), and that is the way he did again. He collected the bones of all five of his children.

Now he went on, he proceeded very very slowly, he went only a short distance. Then he camped overnight. The next day he proceeded again, also very slowly like that. On the fifth day, then he heard them (talking to one another in the basket). They said, "You are lying upon me. Move a little." Then he went along all the more slowly. Now he kept going, he went just a short distance, and then he picked more leaves, he covered it all (with utmost care and constant replenishing with fresh leaves). And that is the way he did as he went along.

She (perhaps a centipede) would run across his path, she would say to him, "Sniff

sniff sniff! (because of the bad odor of decaying flesh) Coyote is taking dead persons along!" He paid no heed to her. Now she ran repeatedly and all the more in front of him, again she would speak like that to him, "Sniff! Coyote is carrying dead persons along!" He laid his basket down very very slowly (with utmost care), he got a stick, he ran after her. I do not know where she went and hid.

Then he packed his carrying basket on his back again, and now he went very very slowly, and he heard his children. Now they were chatting, they were saying, "Move around slowly and carefully! we are making our father tired." Then he was glad, and he went along even more slowly and cautiously. (He walked so very slowly that) he saw his (previous night's) campfire, and then he again camped overnight.

He went on again the next morning, and then that thing (the bug) ran back and forth across his path right there by his feet. Now he became angry. He placed his basket down, and again he chased it. I do not know where it hid.

On the fifth day then he heard them laughing. So he went along even more pains-takingly. Now that thing went still more back and forth in front of him by his feet. He forgot (in his great irritation and tension), he (much too abruptly) loosened and let go his pack basket. "Oh oh oh" his children sounded (and at once died from the shock of the sudden movement of the basket). All done, he finished, and he again put back his basket on himself. When he went along now he did not hear them talking at all. He went along then. They were dead now when he uncovered his basket. Only bones were inside it. He reached his house. The following day then they buried them. He finished (with that effort). He wept for five days.

Then he said, "Indeed I myself did like that (and lost my children because of my doing). The people (who will populate this country) are coming and close by now. Only in that one manner shall it be, when persons die. In that one way had I brought my children back, then the people would be like that (in later eras). When they died in summertime wintertime or toward springtime, after the leaves (came on the trees) they (all the dead) would have come back to life, and such persons would have revived on the fifth day (following a ritual like the one I attempted). But now his (any mourner's) sorrow departs from him after ten days (of formal mourning). Then he can go to any-where where something (entertaining) is happening or they are gambling (and) he may (then shed his mourning and) watch on at it."

Narrative Form as a "Grammar" of Experience: Native Americans and a Glimpse of English

DELL H. HYMES

There is some distance between analyzing texts for patterns of cultural experience and the work of most researchers in child language development who actually observe children acquiring and using language while doing particular things.[1] And yet, I believe that some things which are just beginning to be found out about American Indian myths and texts, particularly narrative texts, have implications for the general study of child acquisition of language. If texts were considered part of a great literature, then in some societies narrative texts would undoubtedly be included in the child's experience of language. These texts turn out to be subtle organizations of lines and verses. The lines and verses are organized in ways that are not only poetry but also a kind of rhetoric of action in that they embody an implicit cultural schema for the organization of experience. These patterns are most finely worked out in myths but can also be found in personal narratives. In the serious and scheduled occasions when children were the specific audience for the telling of myths or when children were simply present when myths or other narratives were being told, not only were samples of language being presented but over and over again, at every level, an implicit organization of experience into set, satisfying patterns was being conveyed and internalized.

For dozens of years we have presented such texts in blocks of prose. There were lines, of course, but these were lines dictated by typesetting and margins on the page. It is not possible to understand what these stories do, and what they are, when you see them that way. I don't rule out the possibility that there are people with minds so subtle and fine that they could actually do it. However, even with languages that I've worked with for twenty years, I can't discern what the stories do and are when they are presented in prose form, so I don't think it very likely that others can. One cannot see the proportions and weighting of the material. One cannot see the relationships among the story elements that show there to be an implicit logic of experience and of literary form.

I would like to give a couple of examples beginning with a rather straightforward example from Zuni, where the telling of myths and personal narratives still goes on a lot today. This is a short story about Coyote, a Trickster hero, and Old Lady Junco, who puts him in his place. The version I'm going to talk about was recorded by Dennis Tedlock and published in his important book *Finding the Center*.[2] It's a fine book and, if you want to get a sense of the life of this kind of literature, it's a wonderful book to look at because the presentation of lines does one of the things that I think is crucial and that is only beginning to be done. It slows down the eye. One reads for form as well as information.[3]

Coyote and Junco

SON'AHCHI.

LO ———— NG A
SONTI GO.

AT STANDING ARROWS
OLD LADY JUNCO HAD HER HOME
and COYOTE
Coyote was there at Sitting Rock with his children.
He was with his children
and Old Lady Junco
was winnowing.
Pigweed
and tumbleweed, she was winnowing these.
With her basket
she winnowed these by tossing them in the air.
She was tossing them in the air
　　while Coyote
Coyote
was going around hunting, going around hunting for his
　　children there
when he came to where Junco was winnowing.
"What are you DOING?" that's what he asked her. "Well,
　　I'm winnowing," she said.
"What are you winnowing?" he said. "Well
pigweed and tumbleweed"
　　that's what she told him.

"Indeed.
What's that you're saying?" "Well, this is
  my winnowing song," she said.
"NOW SING IT FOR ME
so that I
may sing it for my children," he said.
Old Lady Junco
sang for Coyote:

         HINA   HINA
YUUWA   YUUWA

         HINA   HINA
YUUWA   YUUWA

      HINA   HINA
  YU   YU

(blowing) PFFF PFFF

      HINA   HINA
  YU   YU

(blowing) PFFF PFFF

That's what she said.
"YES, NOW I
can go, I'll sing it to my children."
Coyote went on to Oak Arroyo, and when he got there
  MOURNING DOVES FLEW UP
and he lost his song.
He went back:
(muttering) "Quick! sing for me, some mourning doves made
  me
lose my song," he said.
Again she sang for him.
He learned the song and went on.
He went through a field there
and broke through a gopher hole.
Again he lost his song.
Again, he came for the third time
to ask for it.
Again she sang for him.
He went on for the third time, and when he came to Oak
  Arroyo
BLACKBIRDS FLEW UP and again he lost his song.
He was coming for the fourth time

when Old Lady Junco said to herself, (*tight*) "Oh here you come
but I won't sing," that's what she said.
She looked for a round rock.
When she found a round rock, she
dressed it with her Junco shirt, she put her basket of seeds
    with the Junco rock.
(*tight*) "As for you, go right ahead and ask."
    Junco went inside her house.
Coyote was coming for the fourth time.
When he came:
"Quick! sing it for me, I lost the song again, come on,"
    that's what he told her.
Junco said nothing.
"Quick!" that's what he told her, but she didn't speak.
"ONE," he said.
"The fourth time I
speak, if you haven't sung, I'll bite you," that's what
    he told her.
"Second time, TWO," he said.
"Quick sing for me," he said.
She didn't sing. "THREE. I'll count ONCE MORE," he said.
Coyote said, "QUICK SING," that's what he told her.
She didn't sing.
Junco had left her shirt for Coyote.
He bit the Junco, CRUNCH, he bit the round rock.
Right here (*points to molars*) he knocked out the teeth, the
    rows of teeth in back.
(*tight*) "So now I've really done it to you." "AY! AY!"
    that's what he said.
THE PRAIRIE WOLF WENT BACK TO HIS CHILDREN,
    and by the time he got back there his children were dead.
Because this was lived long ago, Coyote has no teeth here
    (*points to molars*). LEE ——— SEMKONIKYA. (*laughs*)

Tedlock and I don't entirely agree on how to analyze narrative texts. In studying oral narrative among the Zunis in New Mexico and the Quiche in Middle America, he emphasizes the oral nature of these texts and the dependence of the organization of these texts upon lines. We both agree that whatever poetry is, in any culture, it is still an organization or grouping of lines according to some patterning. But for Tedlock, the discovery of what these lines might be depends upon hearing the actual voice, listening for pauses, and determining the organization of narrative into lines by the presence of pauses. In other words, each new pause indicates the end of one line and the beginning of another. From a linguistic, theoretical point of view, there is a problem with determining the organization of lines by pauses. If you only have one recording, how do you know that the person would pause in the same place if he told the story again? Also, pauses have to be present, whether motivated by literary concerns or not, simply because no one can tell a four-minute story without breathing. So, the pauses could be an artifact of how long you can hold your breath. They are very likely, then, to be accidental or to be inevitable, and not necessarily a stylistic device. You would have to have repeated tellings of the same story to see the ways in which the patterning of pause was specific to a single story and telling, as opposed to being conventional.

There is another way of organizing the patterning of this story. Every American Indian group has some number which is the number around which a lot of things revolve. If a rite is going to be done a number of times, it will be the sacred number of times, or some multiple of it. Zuni has a pattern number, a sacred number, four. If there are going to be several people in a Zuni story who are brothers or sisters and who follow a course of action, there will be four. If the same thing is going to happen several times until it comes to a climax, it will happen four times, and so on. (Among the Chinookans, as you'll see later on, it's five.) Now it seems to be the case in Zuni that the number four goes with the number two. You'll see that in this little story there's a repeated pattern of "then this/then that."

The story has four parts. In the first part, the two actors are introduced, Coyote and Old Lady Junco. The story says first that she lives here and then that he lives there. The story says that then she was doing this, then he was doing that. He's come to her at the end of part 1. In part 2 she's winnowing seeds. He asks her about the winnowing, and he asks her again about the winnowing. Then he asks her about the song, and she sings the song for him. End of part 2. He now has the song. In part 3, he goes off, loses the song, and comes back. He goes, loses the song, comes back, and gets it again. He goes, loses the song, and comes back, and then, naturally, she should give him the song again, but no. This is where the numerical pattern is not just a mechanical device. You can't just start counting twos and fours and get anywhere. Indeed, what happens here is what happens in some other Zuni stories. The expectation has been built up that this last time will be like the preceding times when she sings it for him again. You're ready for that and it doesn't happen. You're put on hold, dramatically, as she prepares for what will now be the fourth section of the story. This fourth section will be an elaborated double four, an eight-part telling of what does in fact happen the last time. You move up to it, you're ready. And then there's a big surprise. In the fourth part he demands the song, and she doesn't sing. Then he carries out a threat and gets his comeuppance. This takes eight stanzas using the four-part pattern, first by just doing the this/then that, this/then that pattern, and then by saying, "I'll count four times." He gets you through the sixth stanza by the time he's counted the four times, and the last two stanzas are to wrap it up. At the end of the story there is also a reversing of the order of action. Now her action is referred to first, his second; then she speaks first for the first time. The reversal of the turn-taking order signals a reversal of who is in control of the situation.

This is just a short story. According to Tedlock, it took four minutes to tell, which I'm sure is accidental. One could just read it and think it was cute, funny, and amusing. It's the kind of story with a moral point that is often told. By wasting his time trying to learn a song and being no good at it (a shameful failure) both Coyote and his children pay a price in the end. Obviously, to forget a song is no way to behave, but a Zuni would find it amusing to hear of someone who has done so.

There's a rhythm to the story, a subtle patterning of this/then that. The patterning is not talked about anywhere; there are no names for it in Zuni so far as I know. Nevertheless, it's there, just as syntactic relations may be subtly and powerfully present and nobody has a way of referring to them in the native speech community. The child who heard Zuni stories from a person like Andrew Peynetsa, the narrator of this story, was following a kind of logic of patterning that organized the experience into symmetrical, regular relationships. The storyteller also exploited the pattern for effect at the end of the story by putting the audience on hold and then carrying over and doubling the pattern. There's an artistry here that you can't even notice unless you realize this sort of thing is going on in the story. Often the pattern is marked by initial grammatical particles. At certain points the word for *meanwhile* in Zuni (*taachi*) recurs and marks off units. Then the repetition of the word *again* (*taas*) marks off units. But much of it is not overtly marked. Turns of speech also count as units, but most of the words are just part of the actual unfolding of the logic of the event, of a sequence of actions. This is a linguistic point, of course. Many people find that new things are understood about linguistic forms once we look at them beyond the sentence in discourse. This story is an example of that. Given that there does seem to be this internal patterning, the lines of the story could be arranged differently from the Tedlock version. You will see what a difference that makes to the analysis of the text, to the seeing of what is really there.

Andrew Peynetsa's "Coyote and Junco"

[i. Coyote meets Junco]

A   Son'ahchi.
> Sonti Lo::::ng ago:
> At Standing Arrows,
>> Old Lady Junco had her home.

B   Meanwhile Coyote,
> Coyote was there at Sitting Rock with his children,
>> he was there with his children.

C   Meanwhile Old Lady Junco was winnowing,
> pigweed and tumbleweed she was winnowing;
>> with her basket she winnowed these by tossing them in the air,
>>> she was tossing them in the air.

D   Meanwhile Coyote,
> Coyote was going around hunting,
>> going around hunting for his children there,
>>> when he came to see where Junco was winnowing.

[ii. Coyote asks Junco]

A   "What are you doing?"
> that's what he asked her.
"Well, I'm winnowing,"
> she said.

B   "What are you winnowing?"
> he said.
"Well, pigweed and tumbleweed,"
> that's what she told him.

C   "Indeed. What's that you're saying?"
"Well, this is my winnowing song,"
> she said.

D   "Now sing it for me
          "so that I may sing it for my children,"
          he said.
     Old Lady Junco sang for Coyote:
          "Yuuwa hina, yuuwa hina,
          "Yuuwa hina, yuuwa hina;

          "Yuhina, yuhina,
               pfff, pfff (blowing);
          "Yuhina, yuhina,
               pfff, pfff (blowing),"

                    that's what she said.

[iii. Coyote keeps losing the song]

Aa   "Yes, now I can go,
          "I'll sing it for my children."

 b   Coyote went on to Oak Arroyo,
          as he got there,
               mourning doves flew up,
                    and he lost his song.

 c   He went back:
          "Quick! sing for me,
               "some mourning doves made me lose my song,"
               he said.

 d   Again she sang for him.
          He learned the song.

Ba   Again he went on;
          he went through a field there.

 b   Again, he broke through a gopher hole,
          again he lost his song.

 c   Again, he came for the third time
          to ask for it.

 d   Again, she sang for him.

Ca   He went on for the third time,
          again he came to Oak Arroyo;

b   Blackbirds flew up,
    again he lost his song.

c   He was coming for the fourth time.

d   Old Lady Junco said to herself,
    "Oh here you come,
        "but I won't sing,"
            that's what she said.

Da   She looked for a round rock,
    she found a round rock,
        she dressed it with her Junco shirt,
            she put her basket of seeds with the Junco rock.

b   "As for you, go right ahead and ask."
    Junco went inside her house.

[iv. Coyote threatens Junco to his cost]

A   Coyote was coming for the fourth time.
When he came,
    "Quick! sing it for me,
        "I lost the song again,
            "Come on,"
                that's what he told her.
Junco said nothing.

B   "Quick!"
    that's what he told her.
She didn't speak.

C   "One,"
    he said.
"The fourth time I speak,
    "if you haven't sung,
        "I'll bite you,"
            that's what he told her.

D   "Second time, Two,"
    he said.
"Quick sing for me,"
    he said.
She didn't sing.

E   "Three.
        "I'll count once more,"
            he said.

F   Coyote said,
        "Quick sing,"
            that's what he told her.
        She didn't sing.

Ga   Junco had left her shirt for Coyote.

  b   He bit the Junco,
            CRUNCH, he bit the round rock
                right here he knocked out the teeth,
                    the rows of teeth in back.

  c   "So now I've really done it to you."

  d   "AY! AY!"
            that's what he said.

Ha   The Prairie Wolf went back to his children;
  b   By the time he got back there,
                his children were dead.

  c   Because this was lived long ago,
            Coyote has no teeth here.

  d   LEE::::::::SEMKONIKYA. [4]

Recognition of the overall principle of patterning allows us to observe some further niceties of pattern that bear on the relationships between the actors and are part of its aesthetic effect. With regard to the reversal of turn-taking precedence mentioned earlier, notice that there is a symmetry in the story as a whole. Part i begins with Old Lady Junco, and the alternating sequence of actors is J-C-J-C. Part ii begins with Coyote, and the sequence is C-J, C-J, C-J, C-J. Part iii is similar almost throughout, the sequence being C-J, C-J, C-J, J; Old Lady Junco holds the last stanza alone. This anticipates the reversal in the corresponding fourth segment of the next and last part, where Coyote initiates the action for three-fourths of the way (6 stanzas), but Junco is first in their last two exchanges. The sequence here is C-J, C-J, C(J), C-J, C(J), C-J, J-C-J-C. Thus the relationship of the two begins and ends with Old Lady Junco's primacy in form as well as content.

The parenthetic Js in the description of the last sequence are provided because both the logic of the scene and the regularity of the turn-taking imply Junco's silence as response in stanzas C and E. Now, it is in these two stanzas that Coyote goes on to threaten Old Lady Junco by saying how many more times he will count. In stanzas D and F he demands that she sing. And the omission of explicit mention of Junco's response means that she is explicitly said to respond only four times in the overall sequence, twice as not speaking (A, B), twice as not singing (D, F). It is difficult not to believe that the narrator was keeping track of twos and fours in several overlapping respects.*

Now let me turn to a different kind of case. Given what we know about cultural patterns in narratives right now, only a few cases have been looked at from this point of view. I've been working mostly in a corner of the Northwest (in Oregon and Washington) with a language known as Chinookan, whose speakers are almost gone. What we have in the way of texts now is all we will ever have, and yet, as one looks at these stories, one begins to see the effectiveness of this kind of analysis. Looking around that region in the last year or two, I've been able to find this same kind of patterning in a number of different languages adjacent to each other. The stories are full of fives and threes. If somebody acts a series of times, it will be five times. If there is a series of brothers, it will be five. Five seems to be the overall pattern, and three, the one that goes with it. And the two numbers are integrated in a subtle way, a kind of dialectical way. You can get a sequence of five in which the third is the end of the first sequence and the beginning of the next. Thus, five gives you two threes. Now, when I tell you what this means, of course, it's going to sound simple. Doesn't everything have a beginning, a middle, and an end? And yet the stories contain patterns not only at the level of three lines in a row. They contain patterns at the level of three sets of lines in a group, at the level of three larger groupings, stanzas, or whole sections, and at the level of the whole story. So there's a pyramid of this kind of organization. There are twos and fours in the Zuni case, threes and fives in the Chinookan case. The patterns

---

*EDITOR'S NOTE: Dennis Tedlock, in *The Spoken Word and the Work of Interpretation* (Philadelphia: University of Pennsylvania Press, 1983), pp. 57–61, has pointed out in response to this rerendering that his translation "follows the action [and characterization] rather than the demands of versification," embodying Junco's "rather tight voice" and Coyote's "aggressive questioning" (p. 59). Tedlock argues that Hymes's verse-measuring transforms "constantly changing sounds and silences of action into regularized typographical patterns" that appeal to "a symmetry-seeking eye" (p. 61). See Tedlock's new retranslation following the notes to this essay.

are there at every level, yet they are not talked about and have been discovered only recently.

This patterning is also present where something is simply being described. When Coyote is traveling (and he's always traveling), you may say in Chinookan, *gayuya, gayuyaa, gayuyam,* which means "he went, he kept on going, he got there." Or when a boy who is deserted discovers that his grandparents have left him fire so he won't freeze and will survive: "He turned, he looked, he saw the fire." At that level and at every level the same kind of patterning occurs.

In the following Chinookan example, I think you will see also how this patterning works. A little bit about the context and background of this story will be helpful in understanding it. It's a fragment of a story, a fragment which must have been simply a moment of dramatic suspence in a full original version. Throughout Oregon, Washington, and British Columbia, stories have been recorded in which a man or two men seek to revenge either a father or a sister. Brothers revenge a sister, sons revenge a father. In doing so, in order to get into the household of the enemy, they disguise themselves as women, becoming transvestites temporarily. In that disguise they are almost found out, four times if it's a four-part culture, five times if it's a five-part culture. They are almost found out by some little mistake, by not proceeding exactly the way the women they are imitating habitually did. In a few of these stories, the last "almost-discovered moment" is when they're going upstairs to bed where they're going to cut off the head of the man they're after, and a little child underneath looks up and sees in one case a knife hanging down, in another case a penis hanging down and calls out, "This is not a woman." But an older person in the house shushes the child and says not to talk like that. This almost-discovery is frustrated, then, and the heroes (and they clearly are the heroes) successfully carry out the revenge.

Now in this Chinookan text the perspective of the whole story is transformed. All that's left is the episode of suspense just described, and it is told from the point of view of those who are revenged upon, not from the point of view of heroes carrying out revenge. It's told even more subtly from the point of view of the girl who experiences what is wrong and is not attended to. This fragment is worked into a new whole, so that it too has three parts, all told from a single point of view. These things can be seen easily enough if the text is presented in prose form on the page, without recourse to the special organization of lines.

Seal and Her Younger Brother Dwelt There

1. They lived there, Seal, her daughter, (and) her (Seal's) younger brother. I do not know when it was, but now a woman got to Seal's younger brother (and remained as his wife). They lived there.

2. They (all the people) would go outside at night (in order to urinate). The girl would speak, she would tell her mother, "Mother! There is something different (and dangerous) about my uncle's wife. She is just like a man when she goes out (and urinates)." "Do not speak like that! She is your uncle's wife!" 3. They lived there like that for a long long time. They went outside in the nighttime (in order to urinate). And then she would say to her, "Mother! There is something different about my uncle's wife. When she goes outside it (her urinating) is just like a man." "Do not talk like that!"

4. Her uncle and his wife would lie together in bed. Some time afterwards the two of them lay close to the fire, they lay close beside it. I do not know what time of night it was, something dripped on her face (on Seal's observant daughter). She shook her mother. She said to her, "Mother! Something dripped on my face." 5. "Hm. Do not say that. Your uncle (and his wife) are copulating." Presently then she again heard something dripping down. She said to her, "Mother! I hear something dripping." "Oh don't now. Your uncle (and his wife) are copulating." 6. The girl got up, she fixed the fire, she lit pitch, she looked where they (two) were lying in bed. Oh dear oh dear! Blood! She raised her light to it. In his bed her uncle's neck was severed. He was dead. She screamed.

7. She said to her mother, "I told you something was dripping. You said to me, Oh don't say that. They are copulating. I told you there was something different about my uncle's wife. When she went outside she urinated exactly like a man. 8. You said to me, Don't say that!" She wept. Seal said, "Younger brother! My younger brother! They (the house posts in my younger brother's house) are valuable standing there. My younger brother!" She kept saying that. 9. But the girl herself wept. She said, "I tried to tell you but in vain, My uncle's wife urinated not like a woman but just like a man. You said to me, Don't say that! Oh oh my uncle! Oh my uncle!" The girl wept.

10. Now I remember only that far.

This story demonstrates a mode of acting of a mother who insists upon decorum of speech at the expense of actual evidence of experience. That's what the official moral of the story must be, according to the grammar of these things in Chinook. In another way, the story is telling something about the daughter through her experience of wetness. She first hears it, then feels it on her body, and then produces it by crying. In crying the child is assuming maturity. If you look at verbal elements like metapragmatic speech (or metanarrative, as some people call it), you will notice that the mother's speech throughout the myth is a perfect example of Bernstein's "restricted code." [5] It is positional speech in terms of her status as a mother with a certain social position. The girl's speech is not very extensive at the beginning, but the whole last part of the story is turned over to her. She retells the story metapragmatically in an elaborated code and in a burst of elaborated speech so that the story is, in effect, an account of her assumption of a new level of experience and understanding. This is all done in a few lines of the text.

Closer examination, however, reveals important relationship patterns that do not emerge from the text when it is presented in blocks of prose. By presenting the more subtle patterning of lines on the page, we can get a much better idea of the kinds of organization of experience being captured in the story. Compare the block version with this one.

Seal and Her Younger Brother Lived There

They lived there, Seal, her daughter, her younger brother.
    After some time,
        now a woman got to Seal's younger brother.

They lived there.
    They would "go out" outside in the evening.
The girl would say,
    she would tell her mother,
        "Mother! Something is different about my uncle's wife.
        "It sounds just like a man when she 'goes out.' "
"Shush! Your uncle's wife!"

A *long* time they lived there like that.
    In the evening they would each "go out."
Now she would tell her,
        "Mother! Something is different about my uncle's wife.
        "When she 'goes out' it sounds just like a man."
"Shush!"

Her uncle, his wife, would lie down up above on the bed.
    Pretty soon, the other two would lie down close to the fire,
        they would lie down beside each other.

Some time during the night, something comes on to her face.

She shook her mother,
   she told her,
      "Mother! Something comes on to my face."
"Mmmmm. Shush. Your uncle, they are 'going.' "

Pretty soon now again, she heard something escaping.
She told her,
      "Mother! Something is going *t'uq t'uq.*
      "I hear something."
"Shush. Your uncle, they are 'going.' "

The girl got up,
   she fixed the fire,
      she lit pitch,
         she looked where the two were:
            Ah! Ah! Blood!
She raised her light to it, thus:
   her uncle is on his bed,
      his neck cut,
         he is dead.
            She screamed.
She told her mother,
   "I told you,
      'Something is dripping.'
   "You told me,
      'Shush, they are "going." '
   "I had told you,
      'Something is different about my uncle's wife.
      'She would "go out,"
         with a sound just like a man she would urinate.'
   "You would tell me,
      'Shush!' "
      She wept.
Seal said,
   "Brother! My younger brother!
   "They are valuable standing there.
   "My younger brother!"
      She kept saying that.
As for that girl, she wept.
   She said,

"In vain I tried to tell you,
   'Not like a woman,
   'With a sound just like a man she would urinate,
                      my uncle's wife.'
"You told me,
   'Shush!'
"Oh oh my uncle!"
"Oh my uncle!"
   She wept, that girl.

Now I remember only that far.

Throughout the text, relations of threes and fives are organizing what is going on, are making it a satisfying experience, an aesthetic experience, for the narrator and for a native audience. You can see it in the case of the first scene having three parts, each of which begins by saying "they lived there," culminating the third time with "a *long* time they lived there like that." The second scene begins by repeating three times the words "lie down." In the second scene three things also happen. In both the first and second scenes, after an introductory mention of where people are, there follow two exchanges between the mother and daughter, each ending with hushing by the mother. Then there is a final scene which, like the preceding two, begins by specifying where someone is. The girl acts in two verses, each of five lines. In the first, she acts (four times), followed by an expression of what she perceives (a common pattern in American Indian myths). In the second verse, what she perceives is elaborated in three lines, framed by her action and response. These two verses lead to the longest verse of the myth, one central to its interpretation (the girl's long speech of reproach to her mother, accusing her of being responsible for what has happened). This verse has in fact ten lines and five explicit pairings of daughter and mother as addressor and addressee. The frame encloses four reported, enacted speech acts, followed by an end of speech in weeping.

The story takes only a few minutes to tell or read, but its apparent bareness, if skimmed as prose, belies an underlying process of arousal and satisfying of formal expectations of some complexity.[6]

Let me speculate a little about the significance of such findings for language acquisition, first of all with regard to what it may mean in the American Indian case. Such patterns appear again and again, and ultimately we may find them in some form in all American Indian texts. This would mean that the patterns would have been adhered to in formal settings of the telling of myths in winter and in informal storytelling settings as well. Children would have been obliged to listen to these recurring patterns over and over again, in a variety of settings. In Chinookan and other Indian languages there is no explicit way of talking about these patterns, just as there are no words for transformations or the other syntactic relationships of those languages. Yet over and over again, people were being inducted into an understanding of a form of action as a way of organizing experience. In cultures where the telling of stories was a major way of understanding, explaining, and dealing with experience, experience was put into the form of personal or culturally shared narrative. Again and again, instead of a chaos of events, experience was organized into sometimes subtle patterns.

Such organization is very antithetical to major currents in literary criticism in our own society. There, deconstruction and a sort of widespread revolt against stories that have endings and expectable patterns have replaced acceptance of the kind of literary form that took shape for most of the peoples of the world for most of human history. Traditionally, it has been "the arousal and satisfying of expectations," to use Kenneth Burke's definition of literary or poetic form in relation to the audience, that was accomplished through devices such as the ones seen in these Native American texts.[7] Such devices give experience a shape, a satisfying shape which is convincing. As things come out this way, accounts are convincing not only because they may be believed in terms of the actors and actions but also in terms of a form. This form may be hidden in a sense, since no one talks about it, but it is responsible for making the story seem to come out right, to be warranted in the sense of fitting a deep-seated cultural norm for the form of reported experience.

Why would people go to all the trouble? Why not just tell the story of Seal or any other story as a sequence of events: this happened, this happened, then this happened? Why, along with remembering the sequence of incidents and who did what to whom, why also be constantly mapping incidents into an organization of lines, verses, and stanzas that follow hidden, implicit, proportioned relationships? My own speculation, one that may never be provable, is that the North American Indian conception of children made this organization of language very reasonable. Among the Chinookans and some other peoples, children, when they first gave voice, were believed not to be babbling but to be speaking a special language which they shared with Spirits. There were shamans appointed who had the power to interpret this language. The concern was that if the children didn't like it here, they might go back where they were before. The keeping of children was of tremendous importance. Tremendous value was placed on the individual child, and so, in a sense, children were being wooed into adult life. Rather than imagine these communities as living in a simple state of nature where everything is going along as it has to or must, I think one wants to think, at least in part, of people organizing a great literature addressed officially to children. They are the audience. All sorts of terrible things may happen in the stories, but they are addressed to children nonetheless. The children are being inducted into a world which is ordered, in which experience again and again in the form of story, at least, has a recurrent, regular, often multileveled form. Stories always come out in terms of the discourse pattern, regardless of how they come out in terms of the action. There is this invisible, heard-but-not-seen web of order to all experience, or a potential web available for any experience that could become a story. "A cool web of language winds in us," as Robert Graves said.[8] Anything that happens can become a story, and if it becomes a story and gets shaped into the story form, it will have structure just by the carrying out of these principles of patterning, of arousing and satisfying expectation.

This patterning runs so deep that I've begun to find it in unexpected places. When Edward Sapir worked in the west in Oregon in 1905, he was working on a language called Takelma. Sapir was staying with a man who spoke an Athabaskan language called Chasta Costa. When he was there at night, not having anything else to do, he worked on Chasta Costa too and published what little we know of that. He wanted texts, as all good linguists of that generation did, but this man didn't know any stories in Chasta Costa. There was a popular magazine in the house that had some jokes in it, so Sapir got the man to tell him one of the jokes in Chasta Costa. And lo and behold, what did the man do but turn it into a four-part pattern, with turns of talk and everything. It's all there. Thus it seems that this patterning gets carried over even in cases where we would least expect it. I've heard it carried over into conversational English a lot of times. Older people who were raised with these patterns often carry them over when they tell stories of their own experiences in English. We have here not simply a linguistic fact of interest (that sometimes particles and recurrent linguistic items are not boring or monotonous) but examples of particles that actually show structure in narrative discourse. We also have the providing by a culture of an envelope or web of form for all experience, which, at least potentially, is available for inducting children into a kind of cultural security, cognitive and aesthetic simultaneously.[9]

Is this implicit patterning of discourse peculiar to American Indians and not found anywhere else? Well, it's hard to say, for there's so little work as yet in this area. I have looked at some other materials, a few in English. For example, I looked at a couple of the stories that William Labov collected in New York and Courtney Cazden reprinted in an article some years ago; sure enough there's some of this patterning there.[10] I don't think it's as consistent.

The patterning seems more ad hoc, perhaps simply fixing on something like "so" to begin a series of segments of a story, or "like then," or "so then," or "and." To be sure, these elements are not randomly distributed throughout the story but come in sets. They come in clusters, and it may be that "and" is doing the work for a few lines, after which "so then" takes over. Whether there is more to it than that, whether there is a logic or an aesthetic to it, I don't know, but the occurrences are not accidental or random. Again, in some material collected in Gloucestershire, England, by Simon Lichman, of old people telling stories about the revival of mumming tradition, there are recurrences that look a lot like American Indian material.[11] There were two things in particular. First, there is the bringing around of each section of the story to an ending on the same reference point, in this case the Vicar who suddenly overheard the man doing a little step in the garden and found out that mumming was still alive. Second, there is the use of the first word of a line as a point of reference, so that when the man gets to the climax of the story, he has a set of three lines, the first beginning with "that's," and the two that follow beginning with "it's." Now it may be accidental that he chose these three words to be first in each line. But, because they are so similar grammatically and come first, I don't think the choice is accidental. It seems to me that there's a tendency to take advantage of things that come first, especially particles, conjunctions, adverbs, things of that sort. Even in English today, to do a little more with them is not unusual. They show up in threes, fours, or twos, or in sets for one section of a story, then move on to another section.

In our storytelling ability we may be in much poorer shape than the traditional American Indian. We may not have as many good storytellers. Good storytelling gets washed out by all the media and events that influence people's experience with the language. When we do find people lapsing into the performance of a story in which they're really trying to tell it effectively to somebody they know, some of these devices do turn up. We find people using quotatives, which are sometimes thought to be a particularly American Indian device. People use, "He says . . . ," "He says . . . ," to mark off the different sections of a story. Or the beginning sections of a story are marked with "so then," "so then." Or groups are marked by initial "ands" and "buts." Nessa Wolfson has found stories of this sort, although she collected them for a different purpose: namely, to study the occurrence of the historical present in conversational narrative.[12] Looking at stories from the point of view I have been suggesting here, you begin to see that they have sections which tend to be marked off by initial elements which recur in that role. It may be ad hoc to the particular teller or particular story, but it makes me think that this is a general human tendency.

It may be a universal tendency to use words that come first as markers of relationships in stories and to use these relationships to segment stories into sets with lines, or sets with parts. In working with folklore students on their collections of personal history narratives, my wife, Virginia Hymes, has found a considerable variety of devices (tense shifts, among others) marking similar relationships.

In sum, perhaps something that was honed into a truly literary form in traditional American Indian cultures over generations is actually more pervasive than that. For American Indians, the use of words as markers of relationships is also reflected in their English, or it may come out when they are making up a story from a magazine lying on a table. The patterning may not be so pervasive in Boston or Philadelphia, yet it may be something that's partly there, that comes to the foreground in some cases, and that ought to be looked for in more than purely formal features. Patterning may very well bear some of the life of a literary aesthetic impulse in the shaping of experience in narrative, even in today's English and in children's experience of narrative discourse.

The work discussed here is based on the following ideas. First, all oral narrative discourse may be organized in lines. Second, each change of predicate is likely to coincide with a change of line; the distribution of pauses may coincide with the relevant line units, but the fundamental criterion is syntactic, not phonetic. Third, lines are grouped into what can best be called verses. Fourth, the relationships between verses (and often but not always between lines) are grounded in an implicit cultural patterning of the form of action, a logic or rhetoric of experience, if you will, such that the form of language and the form of culture are one and the same at this point. Fifth, such patterning frequently, but not necessarily, is marked by devices at the beginning of lines.

These principles may be universally present but made use of in different degrees and ways. Among American Indian peoples these principles appear to be elaborated into a subtle fabric as principles of literary art, such that performances of myths and even personal experiences may have a subtle fabric. In modern society such principles appear to be present in narrative, as well; the degree to which they are present is yet to be discovered.

What are the implications of these patterns for language acquisition and the teaching of language? Clearly, these findings suggest that the richness of syntax which linguistics finds in every normal child may be accompanied by a richness of narrative organization. The degree to which this is so cannot be assumed in advance. One has to know something of the state of the art of narrative in the community in question, and many communities have been buffeted in ways that erode traditional narrative art. This kind of competence has disappeared from many American Indian communities, as far as the Indian language itself is concerned. Yet patterning may be potentially present in any community's use of language and part of what the child brings to school, at least to some degree.

It is likely that children who have experienced the satisfactions of such patterns in their homes and neighborhoods will find much of what is offered in reading books lacking in interest. There may be conflict between what is assumed by teachers as *the* narrative style and the home-based styles.[13]

It is difficult to say much that is practically pertinent until analyses are made of a range of materials in a variety of communities. Still, it seems safe to say that it is erroneous to think of schooling and writing as necessary sources of the experience of literary form. If, as I believe, the principles that underlie the traditional American Indian artistry are potential in every language, every speech community, democratically ready at hand for everyone, then it would be a sad mistake if these ubiquitous tools were never taken up and used. Modern society does debase local tradition and creativity but does not succeed in eradicating it. Inasmuch as the generative principles of language and narrative are universal, and the need to "traditionalize" experience intrinsic to meaningful human life, we can expect some degree of preschool, and out-of-school, oral narrative experience to be as lasting as humanity itself. Its richness will wax and wane with forces over which schools have no control, but schools will be more effective if they realize its presence and take it into account. Insofar as schools see themselves as outposts of a great tradition, missionaries to their districts, the indigenous oral patterns and potentialities may be factors to be taken into account in transmitting another message. Insofar as schools can see their mission as the etymologically appropriate one of educating in the sense of drawing out, discovery of this kind of patterning can be a source of encouragement and stimulation.

Notes

1. This essay is a transcription of an address delivered at the Sixth Annual Boston University Conference on Language Development, Boston, October 1981.

2. This text is reproduced with the permission of the author, Dennis Tedlock, from *Finding the Center: Narrative Poetry of the Zuni Indians* (New York: Dial, 1972; rpt. Lincoln: University of Nebraska Press, 1978).

3. Kenneth Burke, *Counter-Statement* (New York: Harcourt, Brace, 1931; Berkeley: University of California Press, 1968; Chicago: University of Chicago Press, 1977).

4. "LEE::::::::SEMKONIKYA," the Zunis say, is untranslatable; it is conventionally used to mark the conclusion of a story.

5. Jerome Bruner, "The Social Context of Language Acquisition" (paper presented at the Sixth Annual Boston University Conference on Language Development, Boston, October 1981), published as "Formats of Language Acquisition," *American Journal of Semiotics* 1 (1982); B. Bernstein, *Class, Codes, and Control* (London: Routledge & Kegan Paul, 1971).

6. This story is discussed in detail in Dell H. Hymes, *"In Vain I Tried to Tell You": Studies in Native American Ethnopoetics* (Philadelphia: University of Pennsylvania Press, 1981), chaps. 8–9. The division between scenes 2 and 3 here is different. I had been impressed by finding another Chinookan text (Louis Simpson's "The Deserted Boy," chap. 4 of the same book) to have an elaborated climax in its middle section and thought that the same held here. Certainly there is continuity of action from the mother's "shush" to the girl's getting up, fixing the fire, and so on; and the last three verses of the story, alternating reproach and lament, are a unit. But, as mentioned, the first of these last three verses can be seen as a pivot, ending one sequence of three as it begins another, within a scene of five verses in all. And if one thinks of the story as unfolding in time, it is almost impossible not to imagine that the integrity of the first three verses would carry over for an audience to the next verses, repeating "They lived there" three times (clearly distinct from the next scene of being in bed) and ending as they do on the mother's "Shush." If an introduction and two sets of "Shush" give momentary closure in the first scene, an audience could hardly fail to have a sense of momentary closure the second time the same thing happened: that is, at the end of the sixth verse. The psychologically realistic pattern actually makes more formal sense as well. Each of the first two verses begins with an account of location, as does the third. (Specification or change of location is a common principle of marking initial boundaries in these myths.) Also, the first scene ends with the alternating speech of mother and daughter, as does the third and final scene, as does the second or middle scene.

The girl's major speech is thus not the abrupt beginning of a scene, but the pivotal center of two interlocking sequences of verses. It was right to look for elaboration at the center of a unit, but in this text it comes at the level not of the story but of its final scene.

7. Burke, *Counter-Statement*.

8. Robert Graves, *The Poems of Robert Graves* (Garden City NY: Doubleday Anchor Books, 1958).

9. Dell H. Hymes and Courtney Cazden, "Narrative Thinking and Story-telling Rights: A Folklorist's Clue to a Critique of Education," in *Language in Education: Ethnolinguistic Essays,* ed. Dell H. Hymes (Washington DC: Center for Applied Linguistics, 1980).

10. Courtney Cazden, "The Situation: A Neglected Source of Social Class Differences in Language Use," in *Sociolinguistics: Selected Readings,* ed. John B. Pride and Janet Holmes (Baltimore MD: Penguin Books, 1972).

11. Simon Lichman, "Data on Gloucestershire Mumming Tradition" (unpublished manuscript, University of Pennsylvania).

12. Nessa Wolfson, CHP: *Conversational Historical Present in American English Narrative* (Dordrecht: Foris, 1982).

13. Shirly Brice Heath, *Ways with Words: Ethnography of Communication in Communities and Classrooms* (New York: Cambridge University Press, 1983); Stanley Michaels, " 'Sharing Time': Children's Narrative Styles and Differential Access to Literacy," *Language in Society* 10 (1981): 423–42.

Coyote and Junco [*]

NOW WE TAKE IT UP, NOW WE BE^{GIN LO} ——— NG A_{GO}

•

WHERE THE ^{BOT}TLE GOURD STANDS ON ^{TOP}

OLD LADY JUN_{CO} has her ^{HOME}

and Co^{YO}te

Coyote has his children there at Sitting Rock.

He has his children

and as for Old Lady Junco—

she's winnowing,

pigweed

and tumbleweed seeds, it seems she's winnowing.

With her basket, this way

she winnowed by tossing them in the air.

———

[*]A Zuni story told by Andrew Peynetsa, newly translated (1996) by Dennis Tedlock. *Guide to Reading Aloud:* Pause at least half a second each time a new line begins at the left margin, and at least a couple of seconds for a large dot [•] separating lines. Do not pause within lines, even for a period. Speak more softly than usual for small type and more loudly for CAPITALS. Chant the lines that go up and down (like the first one), with an interval of about a third between levels. Hold a sound followed by a long dash ——— for a second or two.

Peynetsa's performance took four minutes; he learned this tale from a man who had a reputation for telling only very short stories.

Bottle Gourd Stands on Top and Sitting Rock (lines 2 and 5) are a short distance north of Zuni. Old Lady Junco is an Oregon junco, and her shirt or "junco-blouse" (line 24) is the hoodlike area of dark gray or black that covers the head, neck, and part of the breast of this species. The blackbirds are Brewer's blackbirds. "Prairie wolf" (third line from the end) translates *sani,* an esoteric term for coyote, rather than *suski,* the ordinary term.

She's tossing them in the air and Coyote
now Coyote
he's going around hunting, going around hunting for his children there—
he reaches the place where Junco is winnowing.
"What're you DOING?" he says to her. "Well I'm winnowing," she says.
"What're you winnowing?" he says. "Well

•

pigweed and tumbleweed seeds," she tells him then. "I see.
What's that you're saying?" he says. "Well this is my winnowing song," she
    says.
"COME ON, SING IT FOR ME—
then I can
sing it for my children," he says.
Old Lady Junco now
sings it for Coyote,

              HINA   HINA
        YUUWA   YUUWA

              HINA   HINA
        YUUWA   YUUWA

             HINA   HINA
          YU   YU
(blowing)   PFFF PFFF

             HINA   HINA
          YU   YU
(blowing)   PFFF PFFF

she says.
"YES, I, uh, I'M GONE
well I'm going now, I'll sing it for my children."
Coyote went this way, and when he came near Oak Arroyo MOURNING
    DOVES FLY up
and he loses his song.
He came back, he's coming back—
(muttering) "Quick! Sing your song, it was mourning doves, my—
song, they made me lose it," he says.
And now she sings for him,
he learns the song and now he's gone.
This way, where a field is planted then—
and now there's a gopher hole, he breaks through.
And now he loses his song.
And now he comes back for the third time—
he asks for it

and now she sings for him.

Now for the third time he goes and

when he reaches Oak Arroyo,

BLACKBIRDS FLY UP and now he loses his song.

When he came for the fourth time

Old Lady Junco said (*in a tight voice*) "Aw, here you come

but now I won't sing," she says. She looks around for a round rock—

she finds a round rock, she—

puts her junco-blouse on it, she makes her junco-rock look smooth.

(*in a tight voice*) "Go ahead and ask, it's up to you." Junco goes inside her house.

Coyote now comes for the fourth time.

When he comes,

(*muttering*) "Quick! Sing your song," now he's lost his song, so he's back, he
    tells her that.

But Junco doesn't speak.

"Quick!" he says to her, but she doesn't speak.

"ONE!" he says.

"The fourth time I, uh, speak and you don't sing for me, I'll bite you," he
    tells her.

    •

"Second time, TWO!" he says.

"Quick! Sing your song," he says.

When she doesn't sing, "THREE!" he says, "I'll SPEAK for the LAST
    TIME," he says.

    •

Coyote says, "QUICK! SING IT," to her.

She doesn't sing.

Coyote bites Junco clear through.

He bites Junco, CRUNCH! He bites the round-rock Junco.

Right ^here (*pointing to molars*) these ^here all his teeth come out, the whole row
    of teeth comes out.

(*in a tight voice*) "This is exactly what I wanted to do to you." "Ay! Ay!" he
    says.

When the prairie wolf returned to his children, by the time he got there his
    children were dead.

Because of the one who lived this long ago, coyotes have no teeth here

    (*pointing to molars*) e^NOU ——— GH, THE WORD WAS   short.

The Spoken Word and the Work of Interpretation in American Indian Religion

DENNIS TEDLOCK

Our text for this morning comes from the Aashiwi, as they call themselves, or from the Zuni Indians. They live in a town in west-central New Mexico and are now twice as numerous as they were when the Spanish first counted them in 1540. Their language is *shiwi'ma*,[1] one of the 150 languages spoken by the various indigenous peoples of the United States.

The name of the text is *chimiky'ana'kowa*. Literally translated, that means "that which was the beginning." It *is* the beginning, or "that which *was* the beginning." These words were made by what happened at the beginning, and to tell these words is to happen the beginning again. *Chimiky'ana'kowa*.

I speak of a *text*, even though the Zunis do not have a *manuscript* of the beginning. But there is a way of fixing *words* without making visible *marks*. As with alphabetical writing, this fixing is done by a *radical simplification* of ordinary talk. Ordinary talk not only has words in it, in the sense of strings of consonants and vowels, but it has patterns of stress, of emphasis, of pitch, of tone, of pauses or stops that can move somewhat independently of the sheer words and make the "same" words mean quite different things, or even the opposite of what they started out to mean.[2] To *fix a text* without making *visible marks* is to bring *stress* and *pitch* and *pause* into a fixed relationship with the *words*. The Zunis call this *ana k'eyato'u*, "raising it right up," and we would call it chant. In Zuni chant, a strong stress and a high, gliding pitch come into concert on the last syllable of each phrase, or sometimes at the end of a single important word, and are immediately followed by a deliberate silence. All other, weaker stresses occurring between two pauses are equal, and all lower pitches are resolved into a monotone.[3] The number of syllables between two pauses varies from six or seven to twenty or more. This variation has the effect of giving emphasis to the shortest lines, but this is an emphasis *fixed* in the *text* rather than being left to the voice of an individual speaker on a particular occasion. It all sounds something like this (monotone chant, with strong stress and a quick rise on each line—final syllable):

Nomilhte ho'n chimiky'anapkya teya
awiten tehwula
annohsiyan tehwula
ho'na liilha aateyaye . . .

Now in truth our beginning is:
the fourth inner world
the soot inner world
is where we live . . .[4]

The words, or rather the word, of the *chimiky'ana'kowa,* "that which was the beginning," is fixed in a text called *Kyaklo 'an penanne,* the Word of Kyaklo.[5] Kyaklo is a person, a Zuni, who witnessed some of the events of the beginning. He comes once each four or eight years to give his word. He is a stubborn, cranky cripple who must be carried everywhere he goes by the ten clowns who accompany him, and he always demands that the smallest one do it. He always comes into town by the same path, the same path he has followed since the beginning. There is a new subdivision whose streets do not follow his path, so he must be carried through people's yards. There is a house that sits in his path, so he must be carried up over the roof and down the other side. When they come to the river, just before entering the old part of town, he insists that the clowns wade through the ice and mud of the river rather than taking the bridge. He wears the finest clothes, but they always manage to drop him in the river. Kyaklo's face is bordered by the rainbow and the Milky Way, and rain falls from his eyes and mouth. All he does, besides chanting, is to call out his own name: "Kyaklo Kyaklo Kyaklo Kyaklo." The people who want to hear his word assemble in six different ceremonial chambers, or kivas.[6] He carries a duck in his right hand, and if anyone falls asleep while he talks, he hits them with the duck's bill. He goes from one building to the next, still chanting even while being carried through the streets; no one person hears the whole word on one occasion, except for the clowns who carry him. On top of that, he uses a lot of arcane and esoteric vocabulary, so that those who are not well versed in such matters have difficulty in following. Worse than that, he chants rather fast and his words are muffled by his mask. To wear Kyaklo's mask, a person must devote his whole life, for one year, to studying for the part.

So there is our text. Like a cleanly alphabetic text, it consists of a sheer string of words. Kyaklo always pronounces the same words in the same way; it is always Kyaklo chanting, not a particular wearer of the mask. There are no shifts of stress or pitch or pause to find a new meaning, to say nothing of a search for different *words*. Such is the nature of what we call "authoritative texts": they go on saying exactly the same thing, over and over, forever. Any way you look at it, Kyaklo is authoritative text personified.

Now, the *interpretation* of the *chimiky'ana'kowa*, "that which was the beginning," is another matter. The story does not end with Kyaklo. There are fourteen priesthoods at Zuni, charged with meditation on the weather and with divination, and each of them has an interpretation of the beginning.[7] There are thirteen medicine societies, charged with curing, and each of them has an interpretation. And in every Zuni household there is at least one parent or grandparent who knows how to interpret the beginning. I say "interpretation" partly because we are no longer speaking of absolutely fixed texts. The stresses, pitches, pauses, and also the *sheer words,* are different from one interpreter to the next, and even from one occasion to the next, according to the place and time, according to who is in the audience, according to what they do or do not already know, according to what questions they may have asked—even according to what may happen, outside the events of the narrative itself, during this particular telling.[8] Or the interpreter may suddenly realize something or understand something for the first time on this particular occasion. The teller is not merely repeating memorized words, nor is he or she merely giving a dramatic "oral interpretation" or "concert reading" of a fixed script. We are in the presence of a *performing art,* all right, but we are getting the *criticism* at the same time and from the same person. The interpreter does not merely play the parts but is the narrator and commentator as well. What we are hearing is the *hermeneutics* of the text of Kyaklo. At times we may hear direct quotations from that text, but they are embedded in a hermeneutics.

Now, our own phenomenologists and structuralists also quote their texts, removing words from context and even daring to insert their own *italics:* "italics mine." But there is a difference here: the interpreter of that which was the beginning must keep the *story* going. And in this process, the storyteller-interpreter does not merely quote or paraphrase the text but may even *improve* upon it, describe a scene that it does not describe, or answer a question that it does not answer.

The Word of Kyaklo, taken by itself, is a sacred object, a relic. It is not a visible or tangible object, but it is an object nevertheless. What we hear from our interpreter is simultaneously something new *and* a comment on that relic, both a restoration and a further possibility. I emphasize this point because ethnologists, down to the present day, have hankered after the sacred object itself, whenever they could get their hands on it, while devaluing what I am here calling "interpretations." Dell Hymes falls into this pattern when he makes a distinction between what he calls "a *telling about* the story" and "a *doing of* the story" (italics mine).[9] He suggests that we need to gather up the "true performances" from our collections of North American narratives, sorting these out from the mere "tellings," or "reportings," which exist in these same collections. What is stark about this position is that it leaves the "telling about" the story, including commentary and interpretation, entirely up to the ethnologist, while the proper business of the native is limited to the "doing of" the story. This is close to the position of the French structuralists, who limit the native to a narrative or "diachronic" function and concede exclusive rights to the analytic or "synchronic" function to themselves. In effect, the collected texts are treated as if they were raw products, to which value is then added by manufacture.

For the Zuni storyteller-interpreter, the relationship between text and interpretation is a dialectical one: he or she both respects the text and revises it. But for the ethnologist, that relationship is a dualistic opposition. In the end, the text remains the text, still there in the archives and still waiting to be brought to light; the analysis remains the analysis, bearing no resemblance *to* the text and learning nothing *from* the text, and the analyst even takes professional pride in that fact.

The interpretation of the Kyaklo text that concerns us here was given by a man named Andrew Peynetsa, then sixty-two years old, at his farmhouse in the evening.[10] Checking my notes, I find that he gave this narrative over the course of a week in March 1965. He was talking to his wife, one of his sons, his brother, and me. I, of course, had a tape recorder, and my translation from the Zuni follows not only the original words but also the original loudnesses, softnesses, tones, and silences.

Andrew, as a boy, had heard the entire Word of Kyaklo. He and a cousin had been pestering their grandfather to tell a tale, the kind of story the Zunis tell for entertainment. Their grandfather was a cranky old man who didn't really know any tales, but one night he finally consented to tell them something. It turned out to be the Word of Kyaklo. He kept them awake all night, hitting them with a stick whenever they nodded. At dawn he sent them out to do their chores. The next night he resumed his talk, going on all night again. And so on for another night and another, finishing at dawn on the fourth day.

The Zuni beginning does not begin with a first cause; it does not derive an infinite chain of dualisms from a first dualism that in turn springs from original absolute oneness. When the story opens, the earth is already here, the *awitelin tsitta,* literally the "four-chambered mother." There are four more worlds under this one, darker and darker. In this room we're on the third floor, so the bottommost world beneath this one would be a secret basement below the actual basement of this building.[11] Only the Sun Father is up here in this world. Four stories beneath in the Soot Room, in total darkness, are the people. The problem is not to create human beings but that they should be up here in this world, making prayers and offerings to the Sun Father and receiving his daylight, his life. The people down in the fourth room beneath are only *moss people;* they have webbed feet, webbed hands, tails of moss; they are slimy. They do not know what fire is, or lightning, or daylight, or even dawn.

In the Word of Kyaklo and in all previously recorded interpretations, the three rooms between this world and the Soot Room are apparently vacant.[12] This is where Andrew's interpretation introduces one of its elaborations or improvements:

At the beginning
when the earth was still soft
the first people came out
the ones who had been living in the first room beneath.
When they came out they made their villages
they made their houses a—ll around the land.[13]

So the first people out were not ourselves, as in the other versions, but people who were living in the first room beneath this one. But the Sun Father was displeased because "they did not think of anything," they did not give prayers and offerings. When the people in the second room came out, their sulfurous smell, their ozone smell killed all the first ones. They in turn did not think of anything. The people from the third room beneath came out, and their sulfurous smell killed the second people, and they, too, did not think of anything.

Now, the idea that three unsuccessful approximations of human beings preceded ourselves is a common one among Mesoamerican peoples, far to the south of the Zunis. But it is not our concern here to pretend to "explain" the source, the origin of this part of the present narrative. The point is that Kyaklo leaves three rooms vacant, and our interpreter fills them. This may be something "new," or it may even be a restoration of something that Kyaklo forgot. Whatever the case, these first three peoples live and die in a storyteller's *interpretation* and not in the chanter's *text.* They are *not* in the "book."

As we heard before, these previous people "made their villages a—ll around the land." Our interpreter stops for a moment to comment on this:

Their ruins are all around the land as you can see.
Around the mountains where there is no water today, you

could get water just by pulling up a clump of grass

because the earth was soft.

This is the way they lived, there at the beginning.

Not only is this a departure from the official text; it is a departure from the "doing of" the story, and it changes over from third person narrative to direct address: "as *you* can see." Interpretation, here in the form of a small lecture, in the very *midst* of the *text*. It happens again just a few lines later, as the narrator leads us toward the moment when the twin sons of the Sun Father come into existence. It had been raining all night:

Where there were waterfalls

the water made foam.

Well, you know how water can make foam

certainly

it can make foam

certainly

that water

made suds.

It was there

where the suds were made

that the two Bow Priests

sprouted.

There the two Ahayuuta

received life.

Their father brought them to life:

they came out of the suds.

And in another place, having told an episode in which Nepayatamu, the patron of the Clown Society, brings the Molaawe, or corn deities, back into the town after a famine, our interpreter comments:

When the Molaawe enter today

the same procedure is followed:

Nepayatamu

does not speak

when he enters

and the priests are completely quiet inside, well you

have seen this yourself, at the kiva.

Such passages as these raise questions about the relationship of text to world. I mean "world" in the sense that Paul Ricoeur does when he says that the task of hermeneutics is to reveal the "destination of discourse as projecting a world," or when he says that "for me, the world is the ensemble of references opened up by every kind of text." [14] But when the ruins are all around the land, as *you* can see; when *you* know how water can make foam, can make suds; when *you* have seen Nepayatamu and the Molaawe yourself, at the kiva, I don't know whether the text is opening up the world, or the world is opening up the text. This problem is written larger in the narrative as a whole. The world was *already there;* we human beings, or "daylight people" as the Zunis call us, were already there; and, as the narrative details, there were already priesthoods and even a whole village down there in the Soot Room, and the priesthoods were in possession of the seeds of every kind of plant that would grow up here in this world. Still, it is true, we were in the dark, and the world up here on this layer, even if it already existed, had not yet been revealed to us. The Sun Father gave his twin sons the *word* that we were to come out into the daylight, and they brought that *word* down to the priests. The priests responded by setting themselves the very lengthy project of getting us out into the daylight. It looks as though the discourse of the Sun Father had, to paraphrase Ricoeur, projected a world for us. Or, if we follow Ricoeur's recent abandonment of the phenomenological concern with the author's intentions, the Word itself projects a world for us. But "project": that seems like the disembodied ghost of the author's intention, the will of God working itself out in the creation of the world. There is something too inevitable about it all. The word in the Zuni beginning, the word brought by the twin sons of the Sun Father, is *pewiyulhahna,* a word that is *yulhahna: lha-* means important, or even *too* important, *too* much, but the *-hna* on the end makes that negative and the *yu-* on the front puts the word in the indeterminative: *yulhahna,* "sort of not too important," or the word is of "indeterminate importance." It is a word of *some* importance, but perhaps not *too* much.

The Kyaklo text and the available priestly interpretations hint at a general theme of indeterminacy that goes beyond terminological questions, but Andrew's interpretation develops that theme fully. First of all, when the people from the first room emerge into this world, he does not even mention that the Sun Father played any role. When it comes to the second people, the Sun Father simply remarks, "Well, perhaps if the ones who live in the second room come out, it will be good." For the third people, the narrator says, "Those who lived in the third room beneath were summoned"; if it was the Sun Father who summoned them, this is only implicit, but at least we have a glimpse of a will here. Now, we may think, the next stage will be to put the Sun Father and the will together. Here is the way it goes:

The ones who were living in the fourth room
were needed

but
the Sun was thinking

he was thinking
that he did not know what would happen now.

What does happen is the rain, the waterfall, and the sprouting of the twins from the foam. Then we are told, "Their father brought them to life," which points to the operation of will again; but the very next line simply says, "They came out of the suds," and we were previously told that they "sprouted." Whatever is at work here, or *not quite* at work, there is a meeting of the sunlight and the foam of the waterfall, and out come the twins. When the Sun Father tells the twins about the people of the fourth room, ourselves, he says:

You will bring them out, and *perhaps then*
as I have in mind
they will offer me prayer-meal.

"Perhaps," he says, perhaps. The twins say this:

We will *try.*
This place where they may or may not live is *far*
There in the room full of *soot.*

When they enter the fourth room and find the village there, they meet up with a person who happens to be out hunting. This is their first meeting with the *moss people,* the people who are living in total darkness but who are about to receive the Word of the Sun Father, the word that will project a world for them. This hunter they meet is a modest person; he speaks with a weak voice. But before they have explained their project, he remarks,

Well, perhaps I
might know why it is you came.

He takes them to the village, where they meet the Talking Priest, the Spokesman, and give him their "word of indeterminate importance" concerning emergence into the daylight. He responds:

Indeed.

But even if that is what you have in mind
How will it be done?

And he even asks them directly: "*Do you have the means for getting out there successfully?*" To which they respond,

Well

well, no.

The Spokesman then suggests they call in the Priest of the North. But the Priest of the North doesn't know how to get out of the Soot Room and suggests the West Priest. The West Priest doesn't know and suggests the South Priest, and the South Priest suggests the East Priest, and the East Priest says, "I, least of *all.*" He suggests the twins, who brought the word in the first place: "Perhaps they know how to do this after all," he says, and they say,

Well

Well *I don't know.*

But I will *try* something.

The twins take all the people along toward the east for a distance, and then go ahead of them a little. When they find themselves alone, one of them says to the other, "What are we going to do?" And the other makes a further suggestion, prefaced with a "perhaps." With just such questions and perhapses, they manage to find a way up through the third, second, and first rooms. In each room they plant a tree, and the branches of that tree form a spiral staircase into the next and lighter room. But the seeds of all plants were already all there in the dark, in the possession of the priests of the moss people.

When they are all in the first room beneath, where everything is the color of dawn, the twins make an announcement to the people:

Now you must step from branch to branch again

until we come out, out into our Sun Father's daylight. Even

   though it will be hard

you must do your best

to look at your father

for you will hardly be able to *see*

There in the room full of soot, when we entered upon your

   roads, we could hardly *see.*

That is the way it will be with you, *certainly.*[15]

So, just as the Ahayuuta could not see in the Soot Room, the moss people will not be able to see in the daylight. This is the kind of thing that structural analysis is made of. But wait a minute; this is not a trade-off of opposites: "You will *hardly* be able to see," they say to the people; and they say of themselves in the Soot Room, "We could *hardly* see." The hunter they met there said, "Well, perhaps I might know why it is you came"; and the twins, the sons of the Sun Father and the bearers of his Word, said they would *try* something. And when the people finally come out of the last room, they come out not at midday as if expressing a direct opposition between darkness and light, but they come out at the same moment the sun *rises.* It is hard, but they *look at* their Sun Father. At daybreak.

Now the twins take the people eastward for some distance, the first step of a migration that will lead to the place where the town of Zuni now stands. The twins make an announcement:

"*Now*

we will stay here four days," they said. *They were going*

to stay four years.

For four years they lived where they had stopped.

So the twins say four *days,* but our narrator tells us they mean (or the text means) four *years.* Kyaklo does not tell us this, it is *not* in the *book,* but this particular detail is a part of *all interpretations.* It is like the comment of a scholiast in an ancient written text, but it has not become embedded in the text itself. At the same time, it is not set apart in a treatise on theology. It is not the subject of an argument over whether the Book really means seven days. What the Ahayuuta *say* is four *days,* and what they mean is four *years.* But there is something more here than just an explanation, a sort of translation, of the mysterious language of the Ahayuuta. We can't just say, "All right, they really mean four years," and be done with it. It still remains that they *said* four *days.* And if we look again, we see that our interpreter didn't say they *meant* four years. The Ahayuuta say, "We will stay here four days"; and the interpreter says, "They were going to stay four years." But this is not a deviation from *plan,* either. After the four years are up, the Ahayuuta say, "We've been here *four days.*" But I don't want to say, therefore, that they *meant* four years, in some kind of code language. When we decode that, we've got nothing left. We might as well erase "days" and replace it with "years." But our interpreter puts four days *alongside* four years; in fact he does it two different times, once at the opening of this episode and once at the close, just in case we might miss it.

Now, suppose we've heard an interpretation or two of "that which was the beginning," and we finally have an opportunity to go and listen to Kyaklo. When we hear him saying "four days," then we'll know . . . what will we know? Whatever we *think,* he *says* four days. But we can't stop knowing about the four years. Something is happening with time here, within time, something with its marking and its duration, and it is happening *between* the text and the interpretation. It seems like *ages.* It seems like only *yesterday.*

Who are these Ahayuuta, these twins, who talk like this? Their name is a clue because they both go by the same name, Ahayuuta, whereas no two living people should ever have the same name. Once in a great while the Ahayuuta reveal, as they do elsewhere in the present narrative, that they also possess separate names of their own, but they are as close as they could possibly be to the rift between being the same person and different persons. The Kyaklo text and all the interpretations tell us that although they are twins, one of them is the elder and the other is the younger. Of course: twins are born one at a time. But they are as close to the rift of elder and younger as they could possibly be. They are called Ahayuuta *an papa,* "the Ahayuuta's elder brother," and Ahayuuta *an suwe,* "the Ahayuuta's younger brother." They are named by reference to each other. If I refer to the elder brother, I am in effect naming his younger brother "Ahayuuta" and then saying that Ahayuuta has an elder brother. If I refer to the younger brother, I am in effect naming his elder brother "Ahayuuta" and then saying that Ahayuuta has a younger brother. What is called Ahayuuta is between them.

Neither text nor previous interpretations tell us what stage of life these Ahayuuta are in, beyond the fact that they are not fully grown; but now that we can listen to the voice of a narrator as he speaks their lines, rather than merely reading a conventional alphabetic transcription, we hear that the younger one has a high voice that tends to crack.[16] In other words, the two of them are differentiated by the rift of adolescence, even though they were born almost simultaneously.

The twins make everything possible; they are, in Heidegger's terms, "the rift of difference" itself. That rift, he says, "makes the limpid brightness shine," [17] and this is the time to say that the Ahayuuta carry weapons, and that those weapons are lightning. This is their *brilliance.* The people say they are *ayyuchi'an aaho'i,* "extraordinary, amazing beings." *Pikwayina* is the Zuni term for miracle; it means something like "pass through to the other side." If the rain comes through our roof, somehow, and a drop forms on the ceiling and falls, then *k'a pikwayi,* the rain has passed through to the other side. But the Ahayuuta say, "Extraordinary beings we are *not.*" They're a little small for their age, they are dirty, they have lice in their hair. They sprouted from the alkaline foam of a muddy flash flood after a heavy rain. But "their Sun Father brought them to life." Is this their point of *origin?* Is the *will* of the Sun Father the first cause of all differences? Did everything begin with his word? But the world was already there, four rooms of people, already there, these people who might already know something. The Sun Father wants the people to come out of the fourth room, he has a desire in the matter; but he *does not know,* altogether and in advance, what will happen in the meeting of his will with what already is. And from there the Ahayuuta are "given life." Or, they *sprout.* What does it mean to say this is their origin, their starting point? The rain was not made, the earth was not made; they always already were. When we go beyond the Kyaklo text and its interpretations to the *tales* about the Ahayuuta, we again find something that's not in the *book:* in all of those tales, the Aha-yuuta live with their grandmother.[18] Not with their mother—that would be the waterfall, we may guess—but with their mother's mother. They always already have a grandmother. And what is *her* name? She is simply called Ahayuuta *an hotta,* the Ahayuuta's grandmother. Of course. Grandmother of difference. She is the patroness of midwives. And what is her shining? The Sun Father gives daylight and the Ahayuuta travel on lightning. Whenever the Zunis touch a glowing coal to a cigarette, they say they are giving their grandmother a seat in the doorway.

So is *that* the starting of everything? Can we stop here, looking at the face of the Ahayuuta's grandmother? And what is that face? One side of her face is covered with ashes, and the other side is covered with soot. Ashes and fire are already there together. In the live coal, the ashes and soot are not waiting to be projected by the fire. Elder and younger are already there. The Sun and the people are already there. Desire and possibility are already there. The word and the world are already there. The text and the interpretation are already there.

Notes

1. For an explanation of the orthography used here, see Dennis Tedlock, *Finding the Center: Narrative Poetry of the Zuni Indians* (New York: Dial, 1972; rpt. Lincoln: University of Nebraska Press, 1978), pp. xxxiv–xxxv.

2. For a fuller discussion of the nonalphabetic features of the speaking (rather than chanting) voice, see Dennis Tedlock, "On the Translation of Style in Oral Narrative," *Journal of American Folklore* 84, no. 2 (1971): 114–33; and Tedlock, "Oral History as Poetry," *Boundary* 2 3 (1975): 707–26.

3. "Raising it right up" is treated in full in Dennis Tedlock, "From Prayer to Reprimand," in *Language in Religious Practice,* ed. William J. Samarin (Rowley MA: Newbury House, 1976), pp. 72–83.

4. The lines of text and translation quoted here are my own revisions of the version of Matilda Coxe Stevenson, "The Zuni Indians," *Twenty-third Annual Report of the Bureau of American Ethnology* (Washington DC: GPO, 1904), pp. 72–89.

5. Stevenson, "Zuni Indians." This is not a complete version, but it gives a clear enough sense of the texture of the chant. For complete versions of other chants belonging to the same genre, see Ruth L. Bunzel, "Zuni Ritual Poetry," in *Forty-seventh Annual Report of the Bureau of American Ethnology* (Washington DC: GPO, 1932), pp. 710–76. My description of Kyaklo himself draws from Ruth L. Bunzel, "Zuni Katcinas," in *Forty-seventh Annual*

Report of the Bureau of American Ethnology, pp. 980–81, and from my own field notes dating from 1964–72.

6. For a summary of Zuni religious organization, see Dennis Tedlock, "Zuni Religion and World View," in *Handbook of North American Indians,* vol. 9, ed. Alfonso Ortiz (Washington D.C.: Smithsonian Institution, 1979), pp. 499–508.

7. The version of the Priest of the East is given in Ruth L. Bunzel, *Zuni Origin Myths,* in Forty-seventh Annual Report of the Bureau of American Ethnology (Washington DC: GPO, 1929), pp. 549–602; material from pp. 584–602 of this version appears immediately after these notes.

8. For an example of the weaving in of chance events, see Tedlock, *Finding the Center,* pp. 258, 271.

9. Dell H. Hymes, "Discovering Oral Performance and Measured Verse in American Indian Narrative," *New Literary History* 8 (spring 1977): 441.

10. See Tedlock, *Finding the Center,* pp. 225–98, for a full translation.

11. This talk was given on the third floor of the School of Theology Building at Boston University. The Zunis themselves make the analogy between the stories of a building and those of the world. The priesthoods conduct their meditations four rooms beneath the top surface of the main building of the town, in total darkness.

12. See Ruth Benedict, *Zuni Mythology,* Columbia University Publications in Anthropology no. 21 (New York: Columbia University Press, 1935), 1:255–61, for a summary of previous versions.

13. This passage and those quoted hereafter are from Tedlock, *Finding the Center,* pp. 225–98. Each change of line indicates a definite but brief pause, except for indented lines; pauses of two seconds or more are indicated by strophe breaks. In the passage quoted here, "a—ll" is pronounced with a prolongation of both the vowel and consonant.

14. Paul Ricoeur, *Interpretation Theory* (Fort Worth: Texas Christian University Press, 1976), pp. 36–37.

15. The italics here indicate a louder voice.

16. See Tedlock, *Finding the Center,* pp. 168, 177, 179.

17. Martin Heidegger, *Poetry, Language, Thought,* trans. Albert Hofstadter (New York: Harper & Row, 1975), pp. 202–5.

18. See Dennis Tedlock, "The Girl and the Protector," *Alcheringa* 1, no. 1 (1975): 110–50, for a lengthy tale involving the Ahayuuta twins and their grandmother.

Talk Concerning the First Beginning*

Yes, indeed. In this world there was no one at all. Always the sun came up; always he went in. No one in the morning gave him sacred meal; no one gave him prayer sticks; it was very lonely. He said to his two children: "You will go into the fourth womb. Your fathers, your mothers, all the society priests, society pekwins, society bow priests, you will bring out yonder into the light of your sun father." Thus he said to them. They said, "But how shall we go in?" "That will be all right." Laying their lightning arrow across their rainbow bow, they drew it. Drawing it and shooting down, they entered.

When they entered the fourth womb it was dark inside. They could not distinguish anything. They said, "Which way will it be best to go?" They went toward the west. They met someone face to face. They said, "Whence come you?" "I come from over this way to the west." "What are you doing going around?" "I am going around to look at my crops. Where do you live?" "No, we do not live any place. There above our father the Sun, priest, made us come in. We have come in," they said. "Indeed," the younger brother said. "Come, let us see," he said. They laid down their bow. Putting underneath some dry brush and some dry grass that was lying about, and putting the bow on top, they kindled fire by hand. When they had kindled the fire, light came out from the coals. As it came out, they blew on it and it caught fire. Aglow! It is growing light. "Ouch! What have you there?" he said. He fell down crouching. He had a slimy horn, slimy tail, he was slimy all over, with webbed hands. The elder brother said, "Poor thing! Put out the light." Saying thus, he put out the light. The youth said, "Oh dear, what have you there?" "Why, we have fire," they said. "Well, what (crops) do you have coming up?" "Yes, here are our things coming up." Thus he said. He was going around looking after wild grasses.

He said to them, "Well, now, let us go." They went toward the west, the two leading. There the people were sitting close together. They questioned one another. Thus they said, "Well, now, you two, speak. I think there is something to say. It will not be too long a talk. If you let us know that we shall always remember it." "That is so, that is so," they said. "Yes, indeed, it is true. There above is our father, Sun. No one ever gives him prayer sticks; no one ever gives him sacred meal; no one ever gives him shells. Because it is thus we have come to you, in order that you may go out standing yonder into the daylight of your sun father. Now you will say which way (you decide)." Thus the two said. "Hayi! Yes, indeed. Because it is thus you have passed us on our roads. Now that you have passed us on our roads here where we stay miserably, far be it from

---

*Ruth Bunzel, *Zuni Origin Myths,* Forty-seventh Annual Report of the Bureau of American Ethnology (Washington DC: GPO 1929), pp. 584–602.

us to speak against it. We can not see one another. Here inside where we just trample on one another, where we just spit on one another, where we just urinate on one another, where we just befoul one another, where we just follow one another about, you have passed us on our roads. None of us can speak against it. But rather, as the priest of the north says, so let it be. Now you two call him." Thus they said to the two, and they came up close toward the north side.

After similar encounters with six priests representing zenith, nadir, and the four cardinal directions:

"Well, perhaps by means of the thoughts of someone somewhere it may be that we shall go out standing into the daylight of our sun father." Thus he said. The two thought. "Come, let us go over there to talk with eagle priest." They went. They came to where eagle was staying. "You have come." "Yes." "Sit down." They sat down. "Speak!" "We want you." "Where?" "Near by, to where our fathers stay quietly, we summon you." "Haiyi!" So they went. They came to where eagle stayed. "Well, even now when you summoned me, I have passed you on your roads. Surely there is something to say; it will not be too long a talk. So now if you let me know that I shall always remember it," thus he said. "Yes, indeed, it is so. Our fathers, our mothers, all the society priests shall go out standing into the daylight of their sun father. You will look for their road." "Very well," he said, "I am going," he said. He went around. Coming back to his starting place he went a little farther out. Coming back to his starting place again he went still farther out. Coming back to his starting place he went way far out. Coming back to his starting place, nothing was visible. He came. After he sat down they questioned him. "Now you went yonder looking for the road going out. What did you see in the world?" "Nothing was visible." "Haiyi!" "Very well, I am going now." So he went. . . .

The foregoing paragraph is repeated with other birds: cokäpiso, chicken hawk, and hummingbird.

The two said, "What had we better do now? That many different kinds of feathered creatures, the ones who go about without ever touching the ground, have failed." Thus the two said. "Come, let us talk with our grandson, locust. Perhaps that one will have a strong spirit because he is like water." He can go through anything. Thus they said. They went. Their grandson, locust, they met. "You have come." "Yes, we have come." "Sit down. How have you lived these days?" "Happily." "Well, even now you have passed me on my road. Surely there is something to say; it will not be too long a talk. So now when you let me know that, that I shall always remember." Thus he said. "Yes, indeed, it is so. In order that our fathers, our mothers, the society priests, may go out standing into the daylight of their sun father, we have come to you." "Is that so?" Saying this, they went. When they arrived they sat down. Where they were sitting, he questioned them. "Well, just now you came to me. Surely there is something to say; it will not be too long a talk. So now if you let me know that, that I shall always remember."

"Yes, indeed. In order that our fathers, our mothers, and the society priests, may go out standing into the daylight of their sun father, we have summoned you." "Indeed?" Saying this, locust rose right up. He goes up. He went through into another world. And again he goes right up. He went through into another world. And again he goes right up. Again he went through into another world. He goes right up. When he had just gone a little way his strength gave out, he came back to where they were staying and said, "Three times I went through and the fourth time my strength gave out." "Hayi! Indeed?" Saying this, he went. . . . Now as they were sitting around, there the two set up a pine tree for a ladder. They stayed there. For four days they stayed there. Four days, they say, but it was four years. There all the different society priests sang their song sequences for one another. The ones sitting in the first row listened carefully. Those sitting next on the second row heard all but a little. Those sitting on the third row heard here and there. Those sitting last on the fourth row heard just a little bit now and then. It was thus because of the rustling of the dry weeds.

When their days there were at an end, gathering together their sacred things they arose. "Now what shall be the name of this place?" "Well, here it shall be sulphur-smell-inside-world; and furthermore, it shall be raw-dust world." Thus they said. "Very well. Perhaps if we call it thus it will be all right." Saying this, they came forth.

This progress upward continues through successive worlds, soot-inside-world reached by a spruce ladder, and fog-inside-world reached by a piñon ladder. Finally,

passing through to another place, there the two set down their sacred things in a row, and there they sat down. Having sat down, the two set up a cottonwood tree as a ladder. Then all the society priests and all the priests went through their song sequences for one another. Those sitting first heard everything clearly. Those sitting on the second row heard all but a little. Those sitting on the third row heard here and there. Those sitting last on the fourth row distinguished a single word now and then. It was thus because of the rustling of some plants.

When their days there were at an end, after they had been there, when their four days were passed, gathering together their sacred possessions, they arose. When they arose, "Now what shall it be called here?" "Well, here it shall be wing-inner-world, because we see our sun father's wings." Thus they said. They came forth.

Into the daylight of their sun father they came forth standing. Just at early dawn they came forth. After they had come forth there they set down their sacred possessions in a row. The two said, "Now after a little while when your sun father comes forth standing to his sacred place you will see him face to face. Do not close your eyes." Thus he said to them. After a little while the sun came out. When he came out they looked at him. From their eyes the tears rolled down. After they had looked at him, in a little while their eyes became strong. "Alas!" Thus they said. They were covered all over with slime. With slimy tails and slimy horns, with webbed fingers, they saw one another. "Oh dear! is this what we look like?" Thus they said. . . .

Four days—four days they say, but it was four years—there they stayed. When their days were at an end, the earth rumbled. The two said, "Who was left behind?" "I do not know, but it seems we are all here." Thus they said. Again the earth rumbled. "Well, does it not seem that some one is still left behind?" Thus, the two said. They went. Coming to the place where they had come out, there they stood. To the mischief-maker and the Mexicans they said, "Haiyi! Are you still left behind?" "Yes." "Now what are you still good for?" Thus they said. "Well, it is this way. Even though we have issued forth into the daylight, the people do not live on the living waters of good corn; on wild grasses only they live. Whenever you come to the middle you will do well to have me. When the people are many and the land is all used up, it will not be well. Because this is so I have come out." Thus he said. "Haiyi! Is that so? So that's what you are. Now what are you good for?" Thus they said. "Indeed, it is so. When you come to the middle, it will be well to have my seeds. Because we do not live on the good seeds of the corn, but on wild grasses only. Mine are the seeds of the corn and all the clans of beans." Thus he said. The two took him with them. They came to where others were staying. They sat down. Then they questioned him. "Now let us see what you are good for." "Well, this is my seed of the yellow corn." Thus he said. He showed an ear of yellow corn. "Now give me one of your people." Thus he said. They gave him a baby. When they gave him the baby it seems he did something to her. She became sick. After a short time she died. When she had died he said, "Now bury her." They dug a hole and buried her. After four days he said to the two, "Come now. Go and see her." The two went to where they had come out. When they got there the little one was playing in the dirt. When they came, she laughed. She was happy. They saw her and went back. They came to where the people were staying. "Listen! Perhaps it will be all right for you to come. She is still alive. She has not really died." "Well, thus it shall always be." Thus he said.

Gathering together all their sacred possessions, they came hither. To the place called since the first beginning, Moss Spring, they came. There they set down their sacred possessions in a row. There they stayed. Four days they say, but it was four years. There the two washed them. They took from all of them their slimy tails, their slimy horns. "Now, behold! Thus you will be sweet." There they stayed.

When their days were at an end they came hither. Gathering together all their sacred possessions, seeking Itiwana, yonder their roads went. To the place called since the first beginning Massed-cloud Spring, they came. There they set down their sacred possessions in a row. There they stayed quietly. Four days they stayed. Four days they say, but it was four years. There they stayed. There they counted up the days. For four nights and four days. With fine rain caressing the earth, they passed their days. . . . For four days and four nights it snowed. When their days were at an end there they stayed.

The people proceed on to Mist Spring and Standing-wood Spring.

When all their days were passed, gathering together their sacred possessions, and arising, hither they came. To the place called since the first beginning Upuilima they came. When they came there, setting down their sacred possessions in a row, they stayed quietly. There they strove to outdo one another. There they planted all their seeds. There they watched one another's days for rain. For four days with heavy rain caressing the earth. There their corn matured. It was not palatable, it was bitter. Then the two said, "Now by whose will will our corn become fit to eat?" Thus they said. They summoned raven. He came and pecked at their corn, and it became good to eat. "It is fortunate that you have come." With this then, they lived.

When their days were at an end they arose. Gathering together their sacred possessions, they came hither. To the place called since the first beginning, Cornstalk-place they came. There they set down their sacred possessions in a row. There they stayed four days. Four days they say, but it was four years. There they planted all their seeds. There they watched one another's days for rain. During four days and four nights, heavy rain fell. During four days and four nights, the world was filled with falling snow. Their days were at an end. Their corn matured. When it was mature it was hard. Then the two said, "By whose will will our corn become soft? Well, owl." Thus they said. They summoned owl. Owl came. When he came he pecked at their corn and it became soft.

Then, when they were about to arise, the two said, "Come, let us go talk to the corn priest." Thus they said. They went. They came to where the corn priest stayed. "How have you lived these days?" "As we are living happily you have passed us on our road. Sit down." They sat down. There they questioned one another. "Well, speak. I think some word that is not too long, your word will be. Now, if you let me know that, remembering it, I shall always live." "Indeed, it is so. To-morrow, when we arise, we shall set out to seek Itiwana. Nowhere have we found the middle. Our children, our women, are tired. They are crying. Therefore we have come to you. To-morrow your two children will look ahead. Perhaps if they find the middle when our fathers, our mothers, all the society priests, come to rest, there our children will rest themselves. Because we have failed to find the middle." "Haiyi! Is that so? With plain words you have passed us on our road. Very well, then, thus it shall be." Thus he said. The two went.

Next morning when they were about to set out they put down a split ear of corn and eggs. They made the corn priest stand up. They said, "Now, my children, some of you will go yonder to the south. You will take these." Thus he said (indicating) the tip of the ear and the macaw egg. And then the ones that were to come this way took the base of the ear and the raven egg. Those that were to go to the south took the tip of the ear and the macaw egg. "Now, my children, yonder to the south you will go. If at any time you come to Itiwana, then some time we shall meet one another." Thus they said. They came hither.

They came to the place that was to be Katcina village. The girl got tired. Her brother said, "Wait, sit down for a while. Let me climb up and look about to see what kind of a place we are going to." Thus he said. His sister sat down. Her brother climbed the hill. When he had climbed up, he stood looking this way. "Eha! Maybe the place where we are going lies in this direction. Maybe it is this kind of a place." Thus he said and came down. Meanwhile his sister had scooped out the sand. She rested against the side of the hill. As she lay sleeping the wind came and raised her apron of grass. It blew up and she lay with her vulva exposed. As he came down he saw her. He desired her. He lay down upon his sister and copulated with her. His sister awoke. "Oh, dear, oh, dear," she was about to say. Her brother said, "Ah!" He sat up. With his foot he drew a line. It became a stream of water. The two went about talking. The brother talked like Koyemci. His sister talked like Komakatsik. The people came.

"Oh alas, alas! Our children have become different beings." Thus they said. The brother speaking: "Now it will be all right for you to cross here." Thus he said. They came and went in. They entered the river. Some of their children turned into water snakes. Some of them turned into turtles. Some of them turned into frogs. Some of them turned into lizards. They bit their mothers. Their mothers cried out and dropped them. They fell into the river. Only the old people reached the other side. They sat down on the bank. They were half of the people. The two said, "Now wait. Rest here." Thus they said. Some of them sat down to rest. The two said (to the others), "Now you go in. Your children will turn into some kind of dangerous animals and will bite you. But even though you cry out, do not let them go. If, when you come out on the other side, your children do not again become the kind of creatures they are now, then you will throw them into the water." Thus they said to them. They entered the water. Their children became different creatures and bit them. Even though they cried out, they crossed over. Then their children once more became the kind of creatures they had been. "Alas! Perhaps had we done that it would have been all right." Now all had crossed over. . . .

They came (to where the people were staying). "Come, let us go and speak to our children." Thus they said. They went. They entered the lake. It was full of katcinas. "Now stand still a moment. Our two fathers have come." Thus they said. The katcinas suddenly stopped dancing. When they stopped dancing they said to the two, "Now our two fathers, now indeed you have passed us on our road. I think some word that is not too long your word will be. If you will let us know that we shall always remember it." Thus he said. "Indeed it is so. To-morrow we shall arise. Therefore we have come to speak to you." "Well indeed? May you go happily. You will tell our parents, 'Do not worry.' We have not perished. In order to remain thus forever we stay here. To Itiwana but one day's travel remains. Therefore we stay near by. When our world grows old and the waters are exhausted and the seeds are exhausted, none of you will go back to the place of your first beginning. Whenever the waters are exhausted and the seeds are exhausted you will send us prayer sticks. Yonder at the place of our first beginning with them we shall bend over to speak to them. Thus there will not fail to be waters. Therefore we shall stay quietly near by." Thus they said to them. "Well indeed?" "Yes. You will tell my father, my mother, 'Do not worry.' We have not perished." Thus they said. They sent strong words to their parents. "Now we are going. Our children, may you always live happily." "Even thus may you also go." Thus they said to the two. They went out. They arrived. They told them. "Now our children, here your children have stopped. 'They have perished,' you have said. But no. The male children have become youths, and the females have become maidens. They are happy. They live joyously. They have sent you strong words. 'Do not worry,' they said." "Haiyi! Perhaps it is so." . . .

After other adventures with monsters and giants in mountains and caves:

Then they arose. Gathering together all their sacred possessions, they came hither, to the place called, since the first beginning, Halona-Itiwana, their road came. There they saw the Navaho helper, little red bug. "Here! Wait! All this time we have been searching in vain for Itiwana. Nowhere have we seen anything like this." Thus they said. They summoned their grandchild, water bug. He came. "How have you lived these many days?" "Where we have been living happily you have passed us on our road. Be seated." Thus they said. He sat down. Then he questioned them. "Now, indeed, even now, you have sent for me. I think some word that is not too long your word will be. So now, if you will let me know that, I shall always remember it." "Indeed, it is so. Our fathers, our mothers, the society priests, having issued forth into the daylight, go about seeking the middle. You will look for the middle for them. This is well. Because of your thoughts, at your heart, our fathers, our mothers, all the society priests will sit down quietly. Following after those, toward whom our thoughts bend, we shall pass our days." Thus they said. He sat down facing the east. To the left he stretched out his arm. To the right he stretched out his arm, but it was a little bent. He sat down facing the north. He stretched out his arms on both sides. They were just the same. Both arms touched the horizon. "Come, let us cross over to the north. For on this side my right arm is a little bent." Thus he said. They crossed (the river). They rested. He sat down. To all directions he stretched out his arms. Everywhere it was the same. "Right here is the middle." Thus he said. There his fathers, his mothers, all the society priests, the society pekwins, the society bow priests, and all their children came to rest.

Thus it happened long ago.

Poetic Retranslation and the "Pretty Languages" of Yellowman

BARRE TOELKEN and TACHEENI SCOTT

Introduction by Barre Toelken

In recent years, Dell Hymes, Dennis Tedlock, and others have shown how line-by-line presentation of Native American oral literature allows outsiders reading the works in translation a fuller access to the original power and meaning of the stories.[1] This mode of presentation may properly be called "poetic," not because the right margin is uneven or because of any imagined special visual effect but because each line is put forth in such a manner as to render its fullest available charge of texture: rhythm, nuance, phrasing, and metaphor—factors that may depend partly on relation to other lines by parallelism, redundancy, grouping—without forced regard for the printer's convention of justified lines.

Perhaps it is our own literacy that has encouraged us over the years to *see* stories as things, as texts, rather than try to *hear* them as performances. In any case, we have generally been more concerned with efficient translations of texts, no matter how dull the result might be, than we have with renderings of performances, no matter how powerful even a partial success might be. Tedlock's work of translating directly from Zuni into lines showing volume and pitch has demonstrated what *is* possible when oral delivery is recomposed for recognition by the eye. Of course in this process much is lost, but how much is saved can be seen by comparing Hymes's work to Franz Boas's field collections.[2] It is not simply a matter of arranging "regular" oral prose into poetic-looking lines; rather, the translator is forced to deal with the full content in each line without taking refuge in the intellectual, explanatory possibilities of prose rationalization, forced to deal with dramatic directness without a comfortable recourse to indirect description.

Compare the following prose translation given by Boas of the Tsimshian story "The Grizzly Bear" with a poetic retranslation based on Boas's own transcription and interlinear phrase translation.[3] In this passage, the third of three brothers, described as "a great, awkward [perhaps 'improper'] man," has climbed up over a steep icy slope to where his two brothers—one at a time— have been pulled by a grizzly into her den and killed.

> He went near, and had just placed himself in position when the great Grizzly Bear stretched out her arms, and the great man fell into the den headlong. Then he struck the Grizzly Bear and his hand got into her vulva. Then she said to her cubs, "My dear ones, make the fire burn brightly, for your father is cold." She felt much ashamed because the man had struck her vulva, therefore she felt kindly toward him, and did not kill him. She liked him. She said, "I will marry you." And the big man agreed. Then the great Grizzly Bear was very glad because the Indian had married her.

The following "retranslation" uses the wording and phrasing available in Boas's interlinear text of same story. Each utterance is put down here as a separate line; and lines are grouped by topic, action, and import, as defined partly by content, partly by phrasing and parallelism. Admittedly, this is rough guesswork; but even so, a more engaging—I think one may say exciting—dimension becomes available to us: the immediacy of dramatic presence. Added to that, the line-by-line scrutiny helps us recover the line "Then always they lay down," which establishes an important setting of conjugal relationship— left out entirely in Boas's prose translation.

Then he just began to place himself well.
Then suddenly the great Grizzly Bear stretched out her paws.
Headfirst the great man went in.

Then this way he slapped it.
His hand got right into the great vulva
    of the great Grizzly Bear.

Then said the great Grizzly Bear
    to her cubs:
"My dears! Make the fire burn very brightly—
he begins to feel cold,
    your father."

Much ashamed was the heart of the great Grizzly Bear
    because the great man felt in her vulva.
Therefore it was very good for the man
    that she not also killed him
    because inside he had felt.
Therefore she liked him.

Then said the great Grizzly Bear:
"I will marry you."
Then agreed the great man.

Very good in heart was the great woman Grizzly Bear
  because he married her,
  the great Indian.

Then always they lay down.

At the close of the same story, after the bear and the man have gone to live in his village for a considerable time, the Grizzly wife is scolded by a young man who resents her constant presence in the tribal fish trap.

Then the great Grizzly Bear took notice of it. She became angry, ran out, and rushed up to the man who was scolding her. She rushed into the house, took him, and killed him. She tore his flesh to pieces and broke his bones. Then she went. Now she remembered her own people and her two children. She was very angry, and she went home. Her husband followed her, but the great Grizzly Bear said, "Return home, or I shall kill you." But the man refused, because he loved his great wife. The Grizzly Bear spoke to him twice, wanting him to go back, but he refused. Then she rushed upon him and killed him, and her own husband was dead. Then the great Grizzly Bear left.

Following is the same passage, directly from Boas's interlinear presentation, taken line by line. Note how the indirect description and reportage in the rendering above disappear in the dramatic mode.

Then she noticed it,
  the great Grizzly Bear.
Then she came,
  being sick in heart.
Then quickly she ran out at him,
  greatly angry.

Then she went where the man was
  who scolded.
Then into that place she stood.

Then she took the man.
Then all over she killed him.
It was dead,
  the man.
All over was finished his flesh.
Then were broken all his bones.

At once she went.
She remembered her people
    where her two cubs were.
Then went the great Grizzly Bear.
Angry she was,
    and sick at heart.

Then her husband followed her.

Then the Grizzly Bear said this:
"Âdo! Turn back!
Maybe I will kill you!"

Then the man refused,
    because he loved the great wife Grizzly Bear.

Twice spoke the great Grizzly Bear;
    She sent her husband back.

Then he refused.
Therefore she did it,
    the great Grizzly Bear
    rushed back.

Then she killed him.
Then was dead
    the man,
    her own husband.

Then the great Grizzly Bear left.

It was dead,
    the man.

This resetting of the piece does not take into consideration such presentational devices as would surely be discovered by close linguistic scrutiny. Hymes demonstrates, in "Discovering Oral Performance and Measured Verse in American Indian Narrative," that in Chinook stories initial elements such as "Now," "Then," "Now then," are not random conversational connectors but reference points to organizational elements that can be shown in print as "stanzas" and "verses." What is offered here for the Tsimshian story is a rough gathering of passages into scene and action groups, without reference to the richer evidence for even greater meaning and impact which lurks there on the page for someone with language facility to bring forth.

The stark drama of the poetic presentation is obviously more germane to the content and mood of the story's ending than the awkward reportage of the prose account. If it is true, as teachers of literature are wont to insist, that the *way* a thing is said is *part* of what is being said, then we cannot afford to slacken our attempts to determine what those *ways* are in every piece of native literature we seek to study, and what the relationships of those ways are to what is said and meant in each work.

At least it is with this aim in mind that I have encouraged—even forced— my students in recent years to go beyond mere reading of native literature and into the troublesome, frustrating, and often impossible task of recovering something of the original. "But what if we can't *speak* Tsimshian?" they ask. "How are we to presume we can reconstitute the original presentation properly?" My response is to suggest that—using the materials at hand—we can at least come *closer* to a real presentation than is now provided for us in the awkwardly serviceable and often primitive-sounding prose translations of linguists who were less involved in the study of live literature than in the recovery of almost moribund languages.

Throughout this insistence, however, has run one disquieting thought for me: all my own work with Navajo narratives has used prose as the medium of presentation. The one story I have dealt with most fully in print—which has brought positive responses from colleagues and specialists on Navajo language and culture—exists in prose even though my attempt in that article is to reveal the stylistic, presentational aspects of the story. With some trepidation I decided to follow my own advice and retranslate the piece to see what discoveries could be made about the story which *should* have been part of my original discussion. Some of my fears have been borne out: I have discovered patterns, words, and meanings that I did not see before; I have been forced to deal directly with matters that I had easily buried in prose explanation; worst of all, I realized that I had failed even to hear some words because I didn't think they were there. Discussion of the most important of these is presented below.

But first, the following section reproduces, with only minor clarifications, my 1969 essay and prose translation, "The 'Pretty Languages' of Yellowman: Genre, Mode, and Texture in Navajo Coyote Narratives." [4] This is followed by the retranslated text, provided in the poetic line-by-line form. My coauthor and cotranslator, Orville Tacheeni Scott, a Navajo, at the time of our work was a Ph.D. candidate in biology at the University of Oregon. We went through the 1966 tape recording of Yellowman's story several times together; without his help, this retranslation would have been entirely impossible for me. In addition, his elucidation of cultural and linguistic features of the story provided the means of making legitimate and accurate analytic comments that otherwise would have remained unformed.

Toelken's 1969 Article

The story is this: Coyote, wishing to take revenge on prairie dogs for insulting him, persuades Skunk to help him deceive the small animals into thinking he is dead. Prairie dogs are killed and cooked; a race is proposed to see who will eat the cooked animals. Skunk runs out of sight, hides, and returns early, taking all but four small animals up to a ledge where he eats them, later throwing scraps down to Coyote.

Probably no other character is encountered throughout such a broad range of Navajo legend, chant, and folktale as Ma'i (Coyote).[5] Yet even though he has been the subject of scholarly comment in nearly every serious ethnographic investigation of Navajo culture and literature, a close critical analysis of Ma'i in Navajo lore, based on good data, has yet to appear. The scope of such a study is of course far beyond the capabilities of a single essay, or probably of a single writer. Some literary observations on the narratives, however, are possible at this time; because these narratives appear in such a wide spectrum of Navajo tradition, it is obvious even to someone of my limited acquaintance with them that their stylistic attributes reach far beyond the so-called Coyote Tale and into the whole concept of Navajo literary expression.

For purposes of focus here I illustrate my remarks primarily by reference to tales told by one Navajo raconteur. In spite of the severe limitations we must place on generalizing from the data provided by one informant, I would rather work from material I have collected myself (for reasons that will become more apparent below) and from comments made to me by a single good informant than to cope badly with the uncountable critical problems that arise in the use of transcribed texts, no matter how serious or how august their collector may have been. The Navajo propensity to play subtle tricks on outsiders on the one hand, or the occasional attempt, on the other, to apologize rhetorically for the teller's very knowledge of the tales (for example, overuse of the term *jiní,* "they say"),[6] when added to the already dizzying profusion of transcription techniques, makes the close literary use of published texts critically hazardous for anything beyond synopses.

For another kind of focus, directly related to the fact that this is an essay, not an anthology of Navajo tales, I use one particular tale as an exemplar of the literary conditions I plan to discuss. The reader will have to trust my choice of this tale as, first, typical of the Coyote stories and, second, broadly representative of stylistic and structural matters that are not present in every tale but become familiar to one who has heard many of the tales over a period of time. Admittedly, even such brief remarks as I can make here will be a considerable load for such small evidence; the aim of this piece, then, is to be provocative, not definitive. Even so, the observations I make here, as far as I can check them through other data available to me, are not exceptional in nature to those which could be made were I to offer twenty or fifty such tales as textual evidence.

First, a word about the narrator and my acquaintance with him, since these matters have an important bearing on the reliability of the data and on my position as the collector and evaluator of them. It has been my distinct good fortune to have lived among the Navajos on the Northern Reservation (chiefly in southern Utah) off and on for thirteen years, for three of these years under the most intimate conditions, and for nearly all of one year (1955–56) as an adopted member of a family who lived far from roads (in the then remote Aneth district, in Montezuma Canyon) and spoke no English. This was the family of Tsinaabąąs Yazhi (Little Wagon), which consisted of an old man and his wife (in their seventies), their daughter (then about twenty-five years old), her husband, Yellowman (then about forty), and several of their small children. My adoption by the old man put me in the position of participating fully in all the activities of the family.[7]

During a rather severe winter we spent most evenings sitting around the fire in Little Wagon's large hogan listening to the old man tell tales, legends, and miscellaneous yarns. It was under these circumstances that I first observed, albeit unwittingly, something of key importance about Navajo mythic narrative. A small family passing by on horseback had stopped for the night, according to the usual custom. Outside it had begun to snow lightly, and one of the travelers' children asked where snow came from. Little Wagon, in answer, began a long and involved story about an ancestor who had found a piece of beautiful burning material, had guarded it carefully for several months until some spirits (ye'i) came to claim it, and had asked then that the spirits allow him to retain a piece of it. This they would not allow, but they would see what they could do for him. In the meantime he was to perform a number of complicated and dedicated tasks to test his endurance. Finally, the spirits told him that in return for his fine behavior they would throw all the ashes from their own fireplace down into Montezuma Canyon each year when they cleaned house. Sometimes they fail to keep their word, and sometimes they throw down too much; but in all, they turn their attention toward us regularly, here in Montezuma Canyon. When this long story had been completed, there was a respectful silence for a moment; and then the young questioner put in: "It snows at Blanding, too. Why is that?" "I don't know," the old man replied immediately. "You'll have to make up your own story for that." I of course now assumed that the whole story had been made up for the occasion, and so it seemed; but since then I have encountered other students of the Navajos who have heard the same or a similar story. The literary point came to me later, as Little Wagon commented after the travelers' departure that it was too bad the boy did not understand stories. I found by questioning him that he did not in fact consider it an etiological story and did not in any way believe that that was the way snow originated; rather, if the story was "about" anything, it was about moral values, about the deportment of a young protagonist whose actions showed a properly reciprocal relationship between him and nature. In short, by seeing the story in terms of any categories I had been taught to recognize, I had missed the point, and so had our young visitor—a fact that Little Wagon at once attributed to the deadly influences of white schooling.

In these nightly sessions Little Wagon usually held the floor, with his son-in-law, Yellowman, telling only a few tales now and then. It was not until twelve years later, when Yellowman had moved his family to Blanding, Utah (after two desperate years of near starvation on the reservation), that I visited him during the winter when the tales can be told and found him now an apparently inexhaustible source of tales, legends, astronomy, and string figures, narrating almost nightly to his family with a finesse I have not encountered in any other informant. Yellowman has now had thirteen children, and all of those old enough have gone to school. Yet English is not spoken by the children at home; and although Yellowman now lives in a frame house on the edge of town, has made moccasins at the Utah State Fair, works for the Forest Service during the summers, and has numerous contacts with whites, he still prefers not to speak English—probably out of cultural aloofness. He still brings up his children in the Navajo way, still dances in the *Ye'i bichei* Ceremony each year, carries his babies in a cradleboard, and acts the part of cultural adviser to many nearby Navajos. His wife still grinds corn and berries on a flat stone, dresses and weaves in traditional fashion, cooks and serves the usual Navajo fare: coffee, mutton, *náneeskaadí* (a tortillalike dry bread). Because of these and many other elements of cultural conservatism, as well as for his striking talents at storytelling, I consider Yellowman an outstanding and, for our purposes, culturally reliable informant. In addition, he has shown a very cheerful willingness to respond to questions about Navajo stories and storytelling; thus I have been able to check on a number of matters which otherwise would have remained quite indistinct in my mind.[8]

I have mentioned these details at length because they have much to do with the kind of evidence I want to bring forth. Most anthropological data on the Navajos I have read to date are plagued, as suggested partially above, by two great areas of distortion. The first is the well-known tendency of our culture to see things chiefly in terms of its own existing categories, and thus to classify data in its own terms. This leaning may have as much to do with normal thought processes as it does with cultural myopia, and we may never be able to cure it, but we should be aware of its effects on what we suppose to be our objectivity.[9] The second possibility for distortion lies in the Navajo view of information and how it may be transmitted. Sometimes an *attitude* may be accurately communicated in a statement that is technically false but uses humor as a vehicle (such as when an elderly Navajo began to refer to me as his grandfather because of my beard); sometimes aloofness or an unwillingness to be impressed is communicated by statements designed to make the listener appear stupid or to imply that he has missed the point of one's remark (such as when a man heard me say I was from the East—literally, from near where the sun comes up—and commented, as if to someone else, "It must be pretty hot there"); still other information which may fall into a rather large ritual category must be specifically requested four times (the Navajo "special" number), or it will not be given. David F. Aberle found, for example, that some of his information relating to peyotism was affected by his initial unawareness that some potential informants took his single question to mean he did not really want an answer. Very likely he assumed that they were reluctant to answer and, like a gentleman, changed the subject.[10] I cannot safely say that my own work is immune to such problems, or to still others I have not myself isolated or yet recognized; but my firsthand experience with Navajo humor, my presence (and occasional participation) at a good number of Navajo ceremonials, and my continued and ready access to my adoptive family have made me sensitive to such areas when it has come to making generalizations about the data.

With these preliminary remarks, then, let me present a typical "Coyote tale" for consideration here. The narrator's actions, styles, and devices appear in parentheses, the audience's reactions in brackets. These references make it necessary to place information such as linguistic comments in endnotes; since this is at best a burden on the reader, I provide notes only for those points that bear on the story or on the subsequent discussion of it. The story is one I identify descriptively by characters and plot direction, for to my knowledge it has no formal title: Coyote, with the aid of Skunk, plays dead in order to kill and eat some prairie dogs.[11] This particular text was recorded at Blanding, Utah, on the evening of 19 December 1966 as Yellowman told the tale to several of his children; the translation that appears here was made with the valuable help of Annie Yellowman during the summer of 1968.

(style: slow, as with factual conversational prose; regular intonation and pronunciation; long pauses between sentences, as if tired) Ma'i was walking along once[12] in a once-forested area named after a stick floating on the water. He began walking in the desert in this area, where there were many prairie dogs, and as he passed by them they called him mean names, but he ignored them. He was angry, even so, and it was noon by then, so he made a wish:

(slower, all vowels more nasalized) "I wish some clouds would form." He was thinking about killing these prairie dogs, so he wished for clouds, and there were clouds. [audience: smiles and silent laughter]

Then he said, "I wish I could have some rain." [13] He said, "I wish the ground to be damp enough to cool off my hot feet." So the rain came as he wished, and cooled off his feet.[14]

"Now I want a little more, so the water will come up between my toes." [audience: quiet amusement, exchange of glances] Every time Ma'i wishes for something it comes about.

(pause, four seconds) "Now I want the water to come up to my knees." When it reached his knees, he wanted it to be even deeper so that only a small part of his back would show. Then he said, "I wish the water would rise some more so that only the tips of my ears will show." [audience: amusement, heavy breathing (to avoid open laughter)] Now he began to float. Then he said, "I wish I could float until I come to a stop along with some flood debris near the middle of the prairie dogs' area." [audience: quiet laughter] So that happened.

The pile of debris was made up of sticks, pine cones, and other fragments of vegetation, and mud. When he came floating to that place it had stopped raining. Ma'i lay there for a long while, pretending he was dead.

Skunk[15] was on his way by that place to get some water. [audience: silent laughter, knowing looks] Ma'i was pretending he was drowned [audience: quiet amusement] and Skunk didn't know he was there. [audience: open laughter; two girls now giggling almost constantly throughout the rest of this scene] Skunk had a dipper, and put it into the water.

"Shiłna'ash." [16] (Yellowman speaking very nasally, through side of mouth, lips unmoving and eyes closed, in imitation of Ma'i) [audience: open laughter, lasting three or four seconds].

Skunk turned around in fright, but he didn't see anyone. So he put his dipper in the water again, and Ma'i said:

"Shiłna'ash." (nasal, eyes closed, mouth unmoving, as before) [audience: quiet laughter] He said it four times,[17] and on the fourth time Skunk came to that place where Ma'i was lying. (using normal intonation)

(still nasal, lips unmoving, eyes closed, for Ma'i's speech) "Go back to the village and tell the prairie dogs that you were on your way to get water and you came across the body of a dead coyote that got drowned, shiłna'ash. Tell them 'It looks to me like he's been there for some time because it looks rotten and wormy.' Before you go there, get some t'loh ts'osi [18] and stick some under my arms, in my nose, in the corners of my mouth, [audience: mild amusement], in my ears [audience: quiet laughter], in the joints of my legs; tell them how rotten I look. Tell them, 'He must have come down the wash and got drowned.' [audience: quiet laughter] And one last thing before you go there: go make some clubs, four of them, and put them under me. Tell them, 'Since the coyote is dead, why don't we go over there where he is and celebrate?' [19] When they get here, have them dance around in a circle. Keep one of the clubs, and when the prairie dogs beat me with their clubs, you do it, too. When they start dancing and beating, don't forget to tell them to take it easy on me; beat me slowly and not too hard," he said. [audience: laughter]

(normal tone) So Skunk went back to the prairie dogs' village and told the whole story as he was directed by Ma'i. He said, "I was just now on my way to get water and I came across the body of a dead coyote that got drowned. It looks to me like he's been there a long time because it looks rotten and full of worms. He must have come down the wash and got drowned. Why don't we go over there and have a ceremonial to celebrate his death?"

(normal conversational tone, perhaps a bit more slowly pronounced than usual) At the village there were also jackrabbits, cottontails, ground squirrels, and other small animals that Ma'i usually likes to eat. They couldn't believe it. They said (nasal, high pitch), "Is it really true?" "Is it true?" "Is it true?" "I don't know; why doesn't someone besides Skunk go over there and see?" [20] (back to regular discourse, somewhat nasalized) So the jackrabbit went over to where Ma'i was and came back and told them it was all true. Then the cottontail went over there and came back and said it was all true. Then one of the prairie dogs went over there and came back and said, "It's true." On the fourth time they all went over there and gathered around Ma'i to celebrate. They began to dance around him; we don't know exactly what they were singing, but the noise sounded like they were all saying "Ma'i is dead" as they danced around and beat him slowly and gently. As they danced, more of them came along, and Skunk began to get ready to say what Ma'i had told him to say when he said, "Don't forget to do all these things at this time, shiłna'ash."

(nasal whine) Skunk said then, "Look! Way, way up there is a t'ajiłgai [21] far above us." He said it four times, so the prairie dogs all looked up, and Skunk let out his scent [22] into the air and it came down right into their eyes. [audience: laughter] So the prairie dogs were fooled and they were busy rubbing their eyes.

Then Ma'i jumped up and said, "How dare you say I'm dead?" [audience: laughter][23] He grabbed the clubs under him and began to club the prairie dogs. [audience: laughter and giggling] He clubbed all the prairie dogs to death. [audience: extended laughter, including Yellowman (for the first time)]

(pause, after laughter, about four seconds)

"Let's start roasting the prairie dogs, shiłma'ash. You dig out a place in the sand."[24] So Skunk began to dig a place, and build a fire, and he put the prairie dogs in to cook.

"Let's have a race, shiłn'ash. Whoever gets back first can have all the fat prairie dogs." [audience: laughter]

(nasal whine) "No, I don't want to. My legs aren't long enough."

But Ma'i insisted. Skunk complained that he couldn't run as fast as Ma'i, so Ma'i gave him a head start. So Skunk ran off. Skunk ran beyond a hill and hid under a rock.[25] Soon after that, Ma'i passed by, running as fast as he could. He had tied a burning stick to his tail so as to make lots of smoke.[26] [audience: laughter, including Yellowman]

Skunk watched until Ma'i had gone completely out of sight, and then went back to where the prairie dogs were buried. (from this point on until midway in the next scene, the narration gets faster, with pacing related entirely to audience reaction, much in the manner of a "stand-up" comedian in a night club) He dug up all but the four skinniest prairie dogs and took them up onto a nearby ledge. [laughter] And while he was eating he watched for Ma'i, who soon came running as fast as he could. [laughter, including Yellowman] He wanted to make a good finish to show how fast he was, so he came running very rapidly and jumped right over the fire. [laughter, including Yellowman]

"Whew!!" he said. [peak laughter, much extended, including Yellowman] "Shiłna'ash, the poor old man with the stinking urine is still coming along." [extended laughter] Even though he was anxious to begin eating, he didn't want to look greedy, so he paced back and forth in the shade making lots of footprints which would show he had waited for a long time. [laughter, including Yellowman]

Then Ma'i went to the fire and began digging with a stick to find the prairie dogs. He found a tail from one of the small prairie dogs and pulled on it. "Oh oh, the tail must have come loose from being overdone." [laughter] He took out the skinny carcass and threw it over his shoulder toward the east, and said, "There will be fatter ones than this."[27] [laughter]

Now, digging around with the stick,[28] he came onto the second skinny prairie dog and threw it toward the south, and said, "There will be fatter ones here."

(far more slowly, almost drowsily) He came to the third one and threw it toward the west, and the fourth one he threw toward the north. Then he dug around and around with the stick and couldn't find anything. He walked around and around and finally decided to go find those skinny ones he threw away. So he ate them after all. [quiet laughter]

Then he started looking for footprints.[29] [quiet laughter] After a long time he found some tracks leading away from the roasting area to the rock ledge. He walked back and forth along this line several times without seeing Skunk, until Skunk dropped a small bone down from the ledge. [quiet laughter]

Ma'i looked up. (nasal whine) "Shiłna'ash, could I have some of that meat given back to me?" [quiet laughter] He was begging, with his eyes looking upward. [laughter, including Yellowman]

(pause, seven seconds)

(admonishing tone, very slowly delivered) "Certainly not," [30] said Skunk to the begging coyote. He finally dropped some bones down and Ma'i gnawed on them. [moderate laughter]

(pause, about five seconds)

That's what they say.[31]

Lawrence Hennigh has demonstrated the decisive importance of informant commentary in our critical approaches to the understanding of folktales that might seem at first easily classifiable in our terms; his study shows vividly that any consideration of folktale meaning made without reference to the informant's own critical and cultural observations is not only weak but actually invites error.[32] Even though oral informants often disagree on the nature of the same materials, and even though it is probably impossible for a literate, scholarly audience ever to approach an oral tale from an oral culture with anything like a traditional mental "set," no matter how much informant material is available, we still may say that the informant's conception of his own art can open possibilities to us which we might otherwise never suspect, and can save us from the blunder of inserting our own culture's aesthetic prejudices where his belong. With these possibilities and limitations in mind, it is instructive to look into some areas of literary discussion which have come up in my conversations with Yellowman.

For one thing, I had noticed that a good many words and phrases used in the Ma'i stories were not familiar to me from regular conversational Navajo. I had found when I played tapes of these stories to Father H. B. Liebler, a man with some twenty years' fluency in Navajo, that he too missed a good part of the meaning.[33] I asked Yellowman, therefore, if he used a special vocabulary when he told the tales. His answer, not surprisingly, was yes; his explanation was essentially that these were "older" words and phrases, and that he used them because they were the vocabulary he had always heard used in the tales.[34]

But then he added with a smile a comment that I have taken to mean: "They are beautifully old-fashioned." Certainly, the Navajo reverence for beauty and for ancient things is well known, but a slightly new dimension emerged when I talked with Yellowman's children about this matter. They reported that the vocabulary was so familiar to them (they had heard it so often) that they understood it readily, that it did seem to add the valued sense of antiquity to the stories, but that in addition it lent to the narratives a kind of pleasant humor, a comfortable quaintness that seemed to provide (this is my interpretation of their remarks) a ready context for the humorous scenes within the story. The element of humor comes into deeper consideration below.

When I asked if he told the tale exactly the same way each time, Yellowman at first answered yes; but when evidence from compared tapes was brought into the discussion, it became clear that he had understood me to be asking him if he changed the nature of the prototype tale of his own volition; the wording was different each time because he recomposes with each performance, simply working from his knowledge of what ought to happen in the story and from his facility with traditional words and phrases connected, in his view, with the business of narrating Ma'i stories. He did not mention it, but it is quite obvious from tapes made of his stories when no children were present that the audience plays a central role in the narrative style; without an audience, his tales are almost entirely lacking in the special intonations, changes in speed, pacing, and dramatic pauses that are so prominent in the specimen text given above. Speaking in solitude to a tape recorder, Yellowman gives only a rather full synopsis of characters and incidents; the narrative drama, far from being memorized verbatim, emerges in response to the bona fide storytelling context.

Does Yellowman consider these to be chiefly children's stories? Not at all, although he spends more time telling them to his own children than to anyone else. Adults in the audience do not remove themselves; they are as emotionally involved as the children. And, as Yellowman points out, stories of Coyote and his role in the creation, emergence, and placement of stars, and in the continuing fortunes of men and animals, are told during the most serious of adult circumstances (that is, in ceremonies, myth recitations, chant explanations, and so forth) because he is an extremely important personage in the Navajo belief system.

Why, then, if Coyote is such an important mythic character (whose name must not even be mentioned in the summer months), does Yellowman tell such funny stories about him? Yellowman's answer: "They are not funny stories." Why does everyone laugh, then? "They are laughing at the way Ma'i does things, and at the way the story is told. Many things about the story are funny, but the story is not funny." Why tell the stories? "If my children hear the stories, they will grow up to be good people; if they don't hear them, they will turn out to be bad." Why tell them to adults? "Through the stories everything is made possible." [35]

Why does Coyote do all those things, foolish on one occasion, good on another, terrible on another? "If he did not do all those things, then those things would not be possible in the world." Yellowman thus sees Coyote less as a Trickster per se than as an enabler whose actions, good or bad, bring certain ideas and actions into the field of possibility, a model who symbolizes abstractions in terms of real entities. Moreover, Freud notwithstanding, the narrator is in large part conscious of this function.[36] When in one story Coyote loses his eyes in a gambling match or gets them caught on a tree branch during a game, he replaces them with amber pitch balls, and the story ends by explaining, "That's how Ma'i got his yellow eyes." But I exasperated Yellowman on one occasion by pursuing the question of how coyotes could actually see if their eyes were made of amber balls. It turned out just as it had with Little Wagon's snow story: the essence of the tale was not on the surface at all. Yellowman explained patiently that the tale allows us to envision the possibility of such things as eye disease, injury, or blindness; it has nothing to do with coyotes in general; and Ma'i himself may or may not have amber eyes, but since he can do anything he wants to, the question is irrelevant—he has eyes and he sees, period. I have found since then that most Navajos of my acquaintance know the story, with minor variations, and none of them takes it to be etiological.

On the basis of such comments as these (and there are many more like them in my notes), I can suggest several important things: that Coyote tales are not simply entertainment; that they are phrased consciously in such a way as to construct an interesting surface plot, which can act as entryway to a more subtle and far more important area of consideration; that the telling of, and listening to, Coyote stories is a serious business with serious consequences, no matter how much the humor might lead an outsider to feel otherwise; that, in short, the structures and styles we find meaningful in lettered literature are likely to be misleading, or at least irrelevant. I am suggesting that the significant part of the Coyote stories resides in their texture, not their structure, and that excessive attention to structure and stated content may actually stand in the way of our seeing those subtle moral implications and conceptual patterns which seem to be the Navajos' main reasons for telling the story. For one thing, such approaches in the past have led to statements even by strong scholars such as Clyde Kluckhohn, who said of Navajo narratives, "Folk tales are secular in that, although things happen in them which could never occur in ordinary life and are hence part of the supernatural order of events, they are told primarily for amusement and entertainment. . . . Folk tales have none of the high seriousness of the myths." [37] Or the statement by W. W. Hill: "Navajo folklore can be divided into two principal parts: accounts which deal with religious subjects, and stories with morals but which are told primarily for amusement." [38] If both of these do not misunderstand what the Navajos consider a religious subject, they at least do not detect those textural elements which might have connected amusement with religion.

Alan Dundes has suggested that texture in a traditional text is the language employed: the particular phonemes, morphemes, rhymes, stresses, tones, pitches, and so on.[39] I would expand this somewhat and describe texture as *any* coloration given a traditional item or statement as it is being made. In narrative it would certainly include linguistic features, as well as any verbal manipulations which evoke, suggest, and describe, or those which in any way qualify, modify, expand, or focus the rational structure by reference to or suggestion of emotions, mores, traditional customs and associations, aesthetic sensitivities and preferences, and so on.[40]

Dundes is correct in pointing out that "the more important the textural features are in a given genre of folklore, the more difficult it is to translate an example of that genre into another language." [41] And, I would add, the more difficult it is for an outsider even to understand what, in fact, the given item or text means in its own language, and the more difficult it is to delineate genre (since genre, in our culture at least, is usually distinguished on the basis of structure). Admittedly, the concept of genre in our own culture has been cloudy. When we have been able to see clear differences in the way things look on paper (even or uneven right-hand margin) or in fields of focus (novel versus short story), we have been able to make some clear distinctions. But there remains a considerable gulf between those who, like René Wellek and Austin Warren, classify on the basis of form and structure,[42] and those who like Northrop Frye prefer "the radical of presentation." [43] This has complicated our approach to the oral literatures of people for whom the material is not limited to particular forms (especially visible ones) and for whom the radical of presentation is always oral and dramatic.

I found in questioning Yellowman that his own concept of the Coyote materials is based almost exclusively on style, rather than on content or structure. Among other questions, I asked him how he would recognize the difference between a Coyote story and someone talking about Coyote if he were to hear only part of the total text; I asked if it would be possible, by listening to a tape recording, to detect the difference between a Coyote story told within a myth, during a chant, or to someone's family. To the first question, he replied that conversations about Coyote would not use the "ancient" words associated with the tales: at least subject matter is not distinctive. To the second, he replied that Coyote stories would be told about the same way under all circumstances, but that one might detect differing kinds of audience reaction. On these and other topics it became increasingly clear to me that Yellowman sees the Coyote stories not as narratives (in our sense of the term) but as dramatic presentations performed within certain cultural contexts for moral and philosophical reasons.[44] He does not therefore place the materials in separate categories except with respect to the way they are performed; that is, his central consideration is not one of structure/genre but of texture/mode, not because he is unaware of genre (for he distinguishes clearly among song, ceremonial chant, story, and oratory) but because in the case of the Coyote materials generic distinctions are far less relevant than are those textural keys which allow the listeners to gain access to the important levels of meaning.

Following Yellowman's lead here, let us take a closer look at some of the more easily discernible textural elements in the tale presented above. Probably most noticeable are the various recitative devices suggested by my descriptive comments in parentheses. These include a dramatic intonation put on by the narrator as he takes the parts of central characters, especially a slow nasalization of Ma'i's lines; a kind of nasalized delivery of all vowel sounds throughout the story (this may be a part of the "archaism" effect); a variation in phrasing, in which the opening and closing of the story are delivered quite slowly while the climax is in a passage of rapid delivery; the use of appropriate gestures, facial expressions, and body positions in taking the parts of various central characters; and, very important, a kind of contractual interaction developed by the narrator with his audience, which tends to direct these other aspects of recitation and which seems based in their mutual recognition of the story type, its central characters and their importance in the Navajo world view, and their expectation that this particular performance will cause important ideas to come alive in exciting ways.

Another aspect of texture is, of course, language. In this department, without recourse to the special print necessary to make clear the fine shades of oral Navajo, we are limited to a few broad comments. Of basic importance to our understanding of the effect of the Coyote materials on a native audience is the observation that Navajo has no indirect discourse, and it has nothing quite like our infinitive. Thus, one does not say, "He said that he would come"; rather, one says, " 'I will come,' he said." Similarly, in asking whether another needs help, one does not say, "Do you want me to help you?" Instead, one says,

" 'Help me,' is that what you mean to say?" In other words, one must think of how the *other* person would ask it, then say it that way and add *nínízinya?*—which is often translated "you want it?" but really means something more like "Is that what you have in mind?" This is a linguistic feature, not an artistic device; nonetheless, in dialogue where questions are asked, or where information is imparted—especially in scenes where Coyote is trying to trick or take advantage of someone else—this formation, in company with the audience's appreciation and perception of the dramatic context, produces humorous irony. I have already mentioned the intentional use of language patterns for their pleasantly archaic effects on the story, and they need not be treated again here.

There is, between these two areas, another interesting facet of artistic manipulation of a native linguistic feature: in the text above there are three scenes in which there is an unusual overabundance of the nasal *qq* in the words chosen by the narrator.[45] This is a sound that occurs naturally in a number of Navajo words, and one I have heard used widely by itself in informal conversation as an equivalent to the word for "yes": *Aoo'*. Often it is used, in my experience, while someone else is talking, by way of assent, or in order to show that one is listening and following—much like *mhm* in informal English. Its implication, when used alone, is "That's correct" or "I agree" or "Yes, I understand." In the Coyote tales of Yellowman there is a heavy use of words containing this sound in passages where Coyote is illustrating (by observance or nonobservance) some Navajo taboo, in passages where truth is being discussed, and in passages that seem to contain some key action in the development of the story line. There may be other appearances of this device, but I have not been able to catalogue them clearly, mainly because the sound itself is fairly well distributed throughout all the texts I have collected; but suddenly one hears perhaps a whole sentence or as many as three or four sentences that feature this vowel sound almost to the total exclusion of others.

In the tale above the first such scene is the one in which the small animals are trying to determine the truth of Skunk's report of Ma'i's death; the second is the scene in which Skunk hides under a rock and we know he will be the first to claim the roasted prairie dogs (this would be the climax of the surface story and is discussed below); the third use of nasal *qq* comes in strongly as Ma'i begins to exhume the skinny prairie dogs and moves into position for his comeuppance. The impact of such passages is at least threefold. First, on the story (structural) level, we have a morpheme used as part of a word which communicates a particular meaning, with its normal range of denotation and connotation. Second, we have on the "moral" (textural) level a morpheme used to suggest certainty, reliability, "truth" within the local context. Third, we have a complicated set of reactions based on the combination of the other two levels, for while we get a subliminal chant that implies, "Yes, there it is, now we know, this is what they say," we are perceiving simultaneously the irony of the situation—which in nearly every case is based on our recognition that things are not as the story characters see them: Coyote is not dead, a race is not really in progress (and betrayal is at hand), and the gluttonous Coyote gets finally four skinny and sandy prairie dogs. There is, in short, a simultaneous assignment of two different phonemes by use of the same morpheme; since it is done consciously and in particular story contexts, since it is done with the same intent each time (insofar as one can determine such things), and since the effects are quite appropriate to the dramatic context, it is difficult to believe that it happens by accident. The morpheme, nasal *qq*, would seem to constitute a usable, understandable textural formula that establishes a bridge between story and meaning by helping to create irony.

Another great body of textural reference lies in the area of traditional and cultural association: that is, in those words, colors, sequences, and actions which inevitably bring about reactions based on cultural values, mores, customs, and so on. The sequence of fours, as noted above, is—for a Navajo audience—loaded with traditional associations. Not only does a Navajo audience see in the sequence an automatic progression ending on something important at the fourth step, but the ritualism of four-ness in so many areas of Navajo life now carries over to suggest an almost ceremonial significance for the actions of the characters in the tales. More subtle, for the outsider at any rate, is the high incidence of broken customs, or traditions ignored and transgressed. Admission of hunger or tiredness is considered an extreme weakness and is subject to laughter;[46] begging help from someone of lesser talents (as Coyote does in this tale) is idiotic and is subject to ridicule; begging for food is contemptible and brings laughter; any kind of extreme such as overinquisitiveness, obtrusiveness, intrusiveness, gluttony is considered the kind of weakness that must be cured by ceremony and is often in the meantime subject to laughter—especially when it has been carried out by someone who should know better; betrayal in return, if portrayed as a comeuppance in kind, is considered funny. In addition to these considerations, any trick is thought to be funny in itself, no matter by whom or on whom it is played.

If we consider even these few textural possibilities and their presumable impacts on a traditional Navajo audience, and if we play them off against what we see happening on the structural (plot) level, we will find that the structure has acted simply as the vehicle. The structural climax, that point at which we can see the outcome of the story line—that is, when Skunk hides and then doubles back to get the prairie dogs — brings an appreciative look to the faces of the audience, but their heavy laughter begins when Ma'i goes racing by with his self-confident torch blazing. And the heaviest laughter of all comes when Ma'i throws himself down, exhausted, and reveals his weariness by saying, "Whew!!" It is not enough to point out that because the audience has heard the story so many times before it already knows the outcome; after all, the "Whew!!" has been heard many times before as well. What it indicates, I think, is that the audience's attention throughout is on Ma'i, his actions, and his reasons for those actions: that is to say, on culturally moral subjects, which have little to do with "how the story comes out." To put it another way, the attention is chiefly on texture, and the textural climax comes when Ma'i, in a strong symbolic tableau of all the weaknesses and excesses brought out in the narrative, provides a "releaser" for all the laughter that has been built up through the story. What might seem to us a frivolous action not directly related to plot development turns out to be, for the native audience, symbolic of the central concern of the story.

What remains, then, is to posit some relationship between humor, as we have seen it operate above, and "meaning" in the Coyote materials. W. W. Hill suggested that Navajo humor was used in religious contexts in a secondary way, to prevent a "lag in interest," but that humor in "lay stories" was centrally present for amusement's sake. Thus, for Hill, humor in Navajo ceremony was a digression, even though he did note that humorous episodes are often integral parts of ritual acts and in spite of the fact that one informant pointed out to him that "it was not done just because of the fun; it was a part of the ceremony." [47] Hill did, however, recognize something of extreme importance in the social function of Navajo humor: "The difference between ourselves and the Navaho is that in their society institutionalized humor is not a vestigial survival but a functioning organ. Among them humor forms a recognized important adjunct of most formalized social exchange and religious performance." [48] It is unfortunate, it seems to me, that Hill did not follow the ramifications of this idea further, for if humor can be so much a part of religious exercises, it does seem hasty to class all things centrally humorous as "lay" or "secular." It would be illogical to assume that all humor among the Navajos is religious, of course, but we do need to be ready for classifications other than our own.

In the tale above, and in all other Coyote tales I have heard, one is struck by the presence both of humor and of those cultural references against which the morality of Coyote's actions may be judged. We may certainly agree with Hill that the humor does prevent a lag in interest, but far beyond that it functions as a way of directing the responses of the audience vis-à-vis significant moral factors. Causing children to laugh at an action because it is thought to be weak, stupid, or excessive is to order their moral assessment of it without recourse to open explanation or didacticism. What Hennigh says about moral reactions to Eskimo incest tales is exactly applicable here: to enjoy moral defections in a tale, "a listener must be given the opportunity to tell himself, 'I wouldn't do a thing like that.' Thus assured, he can enjoy both the vicarious pleasure of witnessing a tabu being broken and the direct pleasure of moral superiority." [49] Why, though, would one want to feel superior to someone who functions like a deity? What is there about Coyote in particular that he can be both the powerful force he is and the butt of humor in these tales?

First of all, the Navajos did not invent Coyote, as we all know; he is a common character in the tales of many American Indian tribes. Also, as Paul Radin and others have shown, there is something psychologically compelling about Trickster figures that seems to work beyond the local plot structure of any particular Trickster story. These matters have been dealt with amply by others, and I do not propose to open up those topics again here. The real question is how the Coyote stories function within the Navajo view of things in addition to, or in spite of, the universal traits treated by comparatists.

It is important to know that the central Navajo religious ideas are concerned with health and order; very likely, to the Navajo mind, these two concepts are in fact inseparable. Moreover, the kind of order conceived of is one primarily of ritual order—that is, order imposed by human religious action—and for the Navajos this is largely a matter of creating and maintaining health. Health, on its part, is seen as stretching far beyond the individual: it concerns the whole people and is based in large part on a reciprocal relationship with the world of nature, mediated through ritual.[50] The world is seen as an essentially disordered place which may at any time bring bad dreams, witches, encounters with unhealthy animals and situations (lightning, ants), and all sorts of unnamed hazards. Persons may run afoul of nature by not being under control; that is, their natural desires, if allowed full rein, can cause disease (the best example is, of course, excess of any sort). In fact, among the Navajos one common way of envisioning evil is to describe it as the absence of order, or as something ritually not under control.[51] Navajos, in other words, use rituals to establish an island (they might call it a "world") of stability and health in what is essentially— to human view—an unpredictable universe. A Navajo's ability to survive culturally is related directly to an ability to impose the resources of mind, ritually directed, on an otherwise chaotic scene. Nature, of course, is distracting, and in its way fights against regularization. In the myths and stories one finds continual evidence that the concepts of order are continually being challenged (and thereby authenticated in importance) by exponents of that Nature which exists outside humankind. Hill, for example, quoting Washington Matthews's classic account, discusses the clown's antics during the Night Chant: "Thus with acts of buffoonery does he endeavor to relieve the tedium of the monotonous performance of the night. . . . His exits and entrances are often erratic." [52] What he does not mention (and appears not to have known) is that the Night Chant uses what we might call monotony to establish order, and full attention to the entire proceeding is of considerable importance; as with the other rituals, the efficacy of the ceremony is seen as lying in direct proportion to the attention of the participants (which include even the onlookers). Missing a part brings about weakness in the whole. As Gladys Reichard points out of the Night Chant, even within the myth itself inattention to ritual details is dramatically denounced.[53] The clown, then, as far as the serious participant is concerned, does not play the part of a comic reliever but acts as a test, a challenge to order, a living representative of that full world of good *and* evil which exists around us.

I think the position of Coyote in the tales I have been discussing here is roughly analogous to this kind of challenge. If Coyote really were, as Reichard suggests, only the exponent of irresponsibility, lust, and lack of control, his continued central role in moral stories would be puzzling, except, as noted above, for purposes of establishing a sense of moral superiority. But certainly one could feel even more easily superior to a nondeity, if that were all there was to the matter. And why would a deity be, as Reichard describes him, "sneaking, skulking, shrewd, tricky, mischievous, provoking, exasperating, contrary, undependable, amusing, cowardly, obstinate, disloyal, dishonest, lascivious, sacreligious," to quote a few characteristics?[54] Indeed, in her view, Coyote seems almost the demonic opposite of a white Boy Scout (or of a white God, for that matter).

For whatever it is worth, Yellowman sees Coyote as an important entity in his religious views precisely because he is not ordered. He, unlike all others, experiences everything; he is, in brief, the exponent of all possibilities. Putting this together with Yellowman's comment that Coyote makes it possible for things to happen (or for man to envision the possibility of certain things occurring), it seems to me that Coyote functions in the oral literature as a symbol of that chaotic Everything within which human rituals have created an order for survival. Humankind limits (sometimes severely) participation in everything but remains responsive to the exercise of moral judgment on all things and thus uses certain devices to help conceive of order—in this case, stories that dramatize the absence of it. The Coyote materials, then, may be seen as ways of conceptualizing, of forming models of those abstractions which are at the heart of Navajo religion.

It is not off the subject, I hope, to mention that when I lived with Yellowman's family in Montezuma Canyon, I once came down with what appeared to be pneumonia and was diagnosed by a Navajo practitioner as one in need of the Red Ant ceremony. A medicine man (in Navajo, literally, a "singer") was sent for who knew the ceremony, and I was later advised that I was being treated for red ants in my system which I had no doubt picked up by urinating on an anthill. Some time after the ritual (which was quite successful, I must point out) I had occasion to discuss the treatment with the singer: had I really had ants in my system, did he think? His answer was a hesitant "no, not ants, but Ants" (my capitalization, to indicate the gist of his remark). Finally, he said, "We have to have a way of thinking strongly about disease." I now take this to be a ritual counterpart of the functions I have described in the Coyote materials. As ways of thinking and ordering they seem consciously symbolic (but not the less "real" to the users) and much more akin to what I would call artistic modes of thought than to anything we can classify by our normal concepts of genre. At least they are not the simple tales of amusement that so many have taken them for in the past. It would seem difficult indeed to remove them from the total context of Navajo religious thought.

Toelken and Scott's Retranslation

In this line-by-line translation we have tried to come as close as possible to Yellowman's recorded narration while keeping the meaning clear in English. We have endeavored to present each meaningful unit of thought and expression as spoken by the narrator, using his own pauses and phrasing as guides for the lines and verses, and reproducing where possible particularized narrational devices indicating stress, subordination, parallelism, and parenthesis.

Format
Since Navajo is itself a tonal language, the device of multilevel print used by Tedlock for Zuni translations seems inapplicable for indicating stylistic elements of Navajo. Hymes has pointed out, further, that pauses, in and of themselves, may not be clear markers of structural units (like stanzas and verses).[55] We concur in that reservation and use pauses here only as convenient ways to group utterances and keep track of them as units of expression. We leave aside

for the time being the important task of determining whether there are particular and linguistic features that might show these "verses" to have deeper
structural or textural foundation. Thus, the main units of meaning are here
represented as "scenes," larger groupings of actions related to main actors in
the story, carried out in specific locales, as shown below.

Within scenes, lines are grouped by the pacing provided by the narrator.
Compared to other possibilities (topic, grammar, and so on), this seemed to be
a less arbitrary way of dividing the piece into coherent sets of lines, for pacing
and intonation are obviously important and carefully articulated elements of
style for Yellowman, even though his pauses do not constitute neat boundaries
for solid stanzaic definition (for example, some pauses fall in the middle of
ideas). A move from one line to the next indicates the completion of a thought
or phrase as indicated by the narrator's pacing. Utterances too long for presentation in one line are carried over in indented lines; whenever possible, these
indented lines also indicate subordinated or parallel or explanatory elements
where such placement matches the mood of the utterance. Longer pauses than
those between lines (usually less than one second) are used to group lines into
"verses"; the duration of these pauses is shown in seconds between the lines.
Verses are numbered from beginning to end; scenes are designated by capital
letters.

On the right margin appear sparse but important references to narrator style
and audience response. Not much detail is given because these matters were
already discussed in the earlier article. References to the narrator are in italics
and in brackets; descriptions of audience response are in italics only.

Vocabulary

Several words are retained in Navajo because of their special function. Ma'i
as a personage in the story is more important than any biological considerations about coyotes as animals, just as Hamlet as a personage in the play is
more important than the corporeal being or the life and daily affairs of the
person who plays the role. The main difference between Ma'i and Hamlet—in
this regard—is that Euro-American audiences are said to *suspend disbelief* in
watching a play, whereas Navajos can be said to *intensify their sense of reality*
by watching Ma'i.

Although Skunk is not as powerful or ubiquitous a mythic figure as Ma'i,
we retain his Navajo name (Golizhi) so that both main characters can have
analogous reference in the narrative. The term *shiłna'ash* is retained because of
the pointed, humorous irony of its usage; surely the implications of trust, kin-
ship, and interdependence in its translation—"one who walks with me"—are

undercut by Ma'i's use of it in reference to someone he is about to manipulate, cheat, and deprive of food.

Markers

The term *jiní*, "it is said," turns out to be far more heavily used in this rendition of the story than Barre Toelken had earlier thought. Indeed, having encountered it as an apologetic device in some conversations, Toelken offered the confident assurance in the notes to the earlier translation that while one of Edward Sapir and Harry Hoijer's informants had used *jiní* thirty-nine times in a brief version of this story, Yellowman hardly used it at all when narrating directly to his family. On the contrary, the word is used in this text thirty-four times, usually in a contracted form often uttered in a near whisper (*jn*) and thus easy to miss. Believing it was not there, Toelken did not hear it. It occurs most heavily in sections of the story where description is central, least heavily where dramatic dialogue between two characters is taking place.

An important element of meaning totally left out of consideration in the first translation is the intensifier *hááhgóóshįį*. It can be translated in some positions as "very," but most often here it appears before or after a line to establish a sense of importance, intensity of action, urgency, acceleration, or stress for the whole idea. It is the oral equivalent of italics, or of several exclamation points. Although it appears as a word in Navajo, its effect is rhetorical and stylistic. To retain its function without throwing it in as a long Navajo word to confuse matters, we have opted for a symbolic representation: [!!!]. Some speculations on the use of this device are offered below in the critical conclusion. Here it is important to note that the word sounds very much like *hágoshįį* ("okay," "all right") or like *ákoshi* ("and so then"), especially to non-Navajo ears, and particularly when the narrator contracts it to something like *haowshį*, and delivers it in a softer voice than that used for surrounding action words. Toelken subordinated it (and overlooked it in many cases) in the belief that it was a personal redundancy of Yellowman—in the nature of "you know?" in contemporary American English. Thus its role as a means of foregrounding certain key actions remained undiscovered and undiscussed in the earlier translation [!!!], even though style and texture were the intended subjects of the essay.

Another Navajo device lets the reader know that parenthetical explanation or observation is being presented (as in verse 17, where a name for a plant is immediately defined right in the midst of action). Where parentheses appear in the text, they represent Yellowman's formulaic variation in volume and pitch. Brackets in the text, on the other hand, are our device for registering any understood implications or any features of grammar where the total meaning is not susceptible to translation. For example, Navajo has a term for dancing which defines both the shape and motion of the dance and the way people join in; verse 33 shows an attempt to capture it in brackets, but still missing is the movement implied, a regular surging around in unison.

Word Order

Word order, if followed exactly, would make the translation almost totally incomprehensible. Even so, where possible we have retained something very close to the original. Terms such as "he said" and "they say" are used in exactly the same position, for one example. For another, note that the first line of verse 38 starts with a reference to urine, as does the Navajo text, for the stress is clearly on the discomfiture caused by Golizhi's scent, and the mention of urine early in the line maintains the foregrounding of the original. Other attempts are a bit more awkward: verses 30, 31, and 32 try to show the Navajo capacity for combining actions of different kinds, in this case running out and back and reporting on a condition while in transit. The only comfort here is that it would be even more awkward in "standard" English: "The jackrabbit ran over there and ran back, and during his return run reported excitedly that it was true." Given the choice, we took nonstandard awkwardness over standard diarrhea, an attitude that clearly would have benefited the prose translation had it been more bravely applied.

Overview of Scenes and Verses

Just as *King Lear* is not to be described simply as "how a man found out that things are not what they seem," just as *Beowulf* is not "a story about how a young man grew up to be king," so this story cannot fairly be described as a story about "how Coyote tricked Skunk and the prairie dogs and was tricked in return." As the essay attached to the prose translation demonstrates, the story provides important models of world view and morality, and in its evocative texture suggests attitudes and evaluative perspectives on important abstractions of life which relate to health, stability, and order. These concerns do not simply float up out of an uncomplicated plot structure; rather, they cluster in tableau scenes in which particular actors are shown in particular actions in particular places. Following the lead of Melville Jacobs and the applied examples of Hymes, we feel these clusterings can—indeed must—be taken in the nature of scenes or acts in a play: as intentional dramatic interactions played out intentionally on a meaningful stage. These scenes have the effect of spatial or gestural metaphors excited in the minds of the listeners by hearing the particulars "assembled" by a skilled narrator (rather than by watching the assemblage on a stage).

These clusterings are distilled in setting and action, and do not utilize the lineal development in plot which we would normally associate with an "act" in drama; for this reason, we have labeled them "scenes." The opening scene, A, combines a formulaic line (*Ma'i joldloshi lá eeyá*) with a statement that ties Ma'i to a particular landscape and with the narrator's remembrance of *Dinetah*, "Navajo country." The closing formula, I, is not a scene in this same spatial or geographic sense but a rhetorical reference to the cultural setting in which the tale is known and in which it has just been heard and understood. It could as easily be translated, "That's how it happened, they (i.e., we) say."

The scenes may be broken out separately in terms of actor, principal actions, setting, and moral import.

Scene/verse		actor(s)	action(s)	setting	moral topic
A	1–2	Ma'i	trotting	"Where-the-Wood-Floats-Out"	open; potential for recklessness
B	3–17	Ma'i, prairie dogs	running, planning	desert; prairie dog village	anger
C	18–26	Ma'i, Golizhi	running, planning	clump of plants, near water	deception
D	27–32	Golizhi, small animals	running, confirming	prairie dog village; dance	deception
E	33–40	Golizhi, small animals	dancing, urinating, killing	Ma'i's "body"	deception, desecration of the dead
F	41–46	Ma'i, Golizhi	cooking, running, jumping	prairie dogs' bake pit	competition, deception
G	47–58	Ma'i, Golizhi	running, digging	cooking pit; race "offstage"	arrogance, selfishness, frustration, desecration of ritual

| H | 59–62 | Ma'i, Golizhi | pacing, begging | Golizhi elevated, Ma'i below | discovery |
| I | 63 | narrator | recalling | home | participation in culture |

Note that each scene begins with a move toward focus on the particulars of actors, action, and setting while recalling details of the previous scene. These transitional markers (B3, C18, D27, E33, F41, G47, H59) are clear indications of meaningful groupings in the mind of the narrator, and of course they function as powerful directions for the imaginations of the listeners. Moreover, these boundary markers are distinctly different from the continuation-summary device used by Yellowman at the beginning of verse 35, where he takes up the story again after having interrupted his narration for a brief rest. The styles of these two kinds of passages are so different yet so closely related to the "direction" of the narration that they can hardly be coincidental.

Topical Connections

There is a relationship for the Navajos between prairie dogs and rain, probably because the prairie dogs live underground and thus represent the "other side," the reciprocal responses of earth and her inhabitants to the forces that move from the essentially male sky. Similarly, the Hopis connect snakes with lightning and rain. The idea is wholeness, totality; it is not to be shrugged off as erroneous science but experienced as accurate sacred engagement. In one area of the reservation, when a rodent control program was proposed by the government in the 1930s or 1940s, the local Navajos complained, "If you kill the prairie dogs, who will there be to cry for rain?" When older Navajos talk about "the good old days" (that is, before the whites came), they say, "There were prairie dogs all over this area."

Rain relates to fertility (Navajos have a vivid and live sense of this, even distinguishing clearly between Male and Female rain) and thus to food, which is of course a strong central concern in this story. Much of the early part of the story is associated with water (the locale's name, the rain storm, the flood, Golizhi's trip to fetch water); but after Ma'i and Golizhi conspire to deceive and kill the small animals, there is no more mention of water, and Ma'i winds up not with a feast but with only a few bones to gnaw on.

Dances are usually associated with ceremonials that maintain, insure, or restore health, stability, soundness, and "Beauty"; one would not normally think of dancing in celebration of someone's death unless one wanted to suggest the dark and evil side of life encompassed by witchcraft. Neither would one play dead and portray his own flesh as decaying; it would be the direct gestural enactment of everything opposite and counter to the Navajo way of health and long life.

Betrayals and outright lying are frowned upon, although one often encounters them in jokes and tricks. Playing jokes on people is a common pastime among the Navajos, so the logic of pretending in this story is of course deliciously funny to a Navajo audience. But jokes of this sort? Jokes that end in competition for food instead of reciprocation, that end in death, that feature a betrayal of one's partner? These jokes are very much in the category of traveling salesman jokes for Anglo-Americans, for they encapsulate exactly those actions which are *not* supposed to take place in real life, which cause us anxiety even to think about. The narrative provides us, among other things, with a way of projecting and experiencing our anxieties. To Navajos, serious and repeated lying, extreme irritability, impatience, open frustration, compulsive competition, and the breaking of taboos are all seen as symptomatic of illness, and illness is a big concern for everyone nearby. In brief, nearly every action in this story, seen in its moral frame, is "wrong" in a traditional sense, even though within the narrative frame each action has its own internal logic, especially given the well-known unpredictable aspect of Ma'i's personality.

A   (1)   Ma'i was trotting along [having always done so].   [*slowly*]

             -4-

     (2)   At a place I'm not familiar with called "Where the Wood Floats
            Out" he was walking along, it is said.

             -4-

B   (3)   Then, also in an open area, it is said [!!!],
            he was walking along in the midst of many prairie dogs [!!!].

             -1-

     (4)   [!!!] The prairie dogs were cursing him, it is said [!!!],
            all crowded together, yelling.

             -1-

     (5)   He went along further into their midst.

             -1-

     (6)   Then he walked further.

             -3-

     (7)   [!!!] He got angry and soon began to feel hostile.

             -2-

     (8)   After a while it was noon.

             -1-

(9) He wanted [implied: looking upward] a cloud   *[slower, nasal]*
        to appear
     (His reason was that he started hating the prairie dogs),
        so he asked for rain.
                             -2-   *smiles, quiet laughter*

(10) Then a cloud appeared, it is said.
     "If it would only rain on me," he said.   *smiles, heavy breathing*
     And that's what happened, it is said.
                             -2-

(11) "If only there could be rain in my footprints."
     And that's what happened, it is said.
     "If only water would ooze up between my toes
        as I walk along," he said.
                             -3-   *open amusement*

(12) Then everything happened as he said, it is said.
                             -4-   *[clears throat]*

(13) "If only the water would come up to my knees," he said.
     And that's what happened.
                             -2-

(14) "If only the water would be up to my back
        so that only my ears would be out of the water."   *[nasal]*
                             -13-   *heavy breathing; baby cries*

(15) "If I could only float," he said.   *[nasal]*
     Then, starting to float,
     "Where the prairie dogs are,
        if I could only land there," he said.
                             -3-   *quiet laughter*

(16) He came to rest in the midst of the prairie dog town, it is said.
                             -3-

(17) Someplace in the *diz*—   *smiles, quiet laughter*
        (*diz* is the name of a plant that grows in clumps)—
     he landed [implied: along with other debris] hung up
        in the clump, it is said.
                             -4-   *quiet laughter*

C (18) And there he was lying after the rain.
        And then Golizhi was running by to fetch water.   *[slower]*
           (Ma'i was pretending to be dead)   *smiles exchanged*
        Then he [Golizhi] was running.   *glances*

He [Ma'i] called out to him, it is said.

"Come here," he said, and Golizhi came to him,   [*very nasal*]
     it is said.

                        -6-   *suppressed giggling*

(19) "Shiłna'ash," he said [very seriously].   [*nasal*]

                        -2-   *quiet laughter, expelling air*

(20) " 'The hated one has died, and has washed up   [*nasal*]
     where the prairie dogs are,' tell them that, shiłna'ash."

                        -3-

(21) " 'He's already got maggots,' you tell them," he said.   [*nasal*]

                        -2-

(22) "Slendergrass, it is called—shake that Slendergrass
     so the seeds fall off.

In my crotch, in my nose, in the back part of my mouth,
     scatter some around, then put some inside my ears," he said.

" 'He's got maggots,' you tell them.   *quiet laughter*
'The hated one has been washed out.' "

                        -3-   *quiet laughter*

(23) "Make four clubs and put them under me.

                        -3-

(24) 'We'll dance over him.
We're all going to meet over there,'
     you tell them," he said.

                        -1-

(25) "This is how," he said.
. . . . [wording indistinct] . . . .
. . . . "dancing around" . . .
[implied: Golizhi is to join in these actions]
. . . " 'Hit Ma'i in the ribs' " . . . .   *breathing*

                        -1-

(26) "Be careful not to hit me too hard!
'Slowly, gently, like this,'   *laughter*
     you tell them," he said.

                        -5-   [*clears throat*]

D (27) This happened.   [*normal tone*]
He ran home, and gave out the word to the prairie dogs, it is said.
"The hated one is washed out [!!!]."

                        -2-

(28) There were rabbits and other animals [there],
          and even groundsquirrels.
      (Those animals which are food for him were gathered [!!!].)
      [!!!] Now the people were dancing, it is said, at the meeting.
                          -3-

(29) First, he [Golizhi] said, "It's true! It's true!   *[tones exaggerated]*
      Let's have one of you who runs fast run over there to find out."
                          -1-

(30) Then Jackrabbit ran and, "It's true!" said,   *quiet giggling*
          running back, it is said.
                          -1-

(31) Then Cottontail ran and, "It's true!" said,
          running back, it is said.
                          -1-

(32) Then Prairie dog ran and, they say, "It's true!" said,
          running back, it is said.
                          -1-

E (33) At that time there was a big gathering [!!!].
      They were dancing [implied: couples periodically stepping into circle],
          it is said.
      Whatever they were singing, I don't know.
                          -2-

(34) "The hated one is dead," they were saying [!!!];
          the club is beside him; they were hitting
          him in the ribs, it is said.   *[delivered in one long breath]*
                      -rest-   *expelling of air*
      —*[narrator rests for about five minutes, drinks coffee]*—

(35) Then they continued with what they were doing,
          and more and more people came.
      Then Golizhi-ye-ne said (remembering Ma'i's plan)
      "You are all dancing;
      While you are looking up, while you are saying,
          you say 'Dance in that manner,' you tell them [!!!]
          'while you're in charge there, shiłna'ash,' he said."
                          -2-

(36) Then they were dancing.
      Then, "Waay, waay up there a *t'aadziłgai* is running through the
          air," he said,
          Golizhi said.   *one girl: hn!*

-1-
(37) Then, when they were all looking up,
    he urinated upward
        so that it fell in their eyes, the urine.

        -3-   *open laughter*
(38) His urine the animals were rubbing from their eyes [!!!].
    " 'The one who is hated is dead?' " he [Ma'i] said, jumping up [!!!].

        -1-   *laughter, giggling*
(39) He grabbed the clubs from under him [!!!].

        -3-   *laughter, giggling*
(40) He used the clubs on them [all in a row, in one circular swing].
    They were all clubbed to death.   *[laughter]*

        -8-   *laughter*
F (41) Then,
    "Let us cook by burying, shiłna'ash," he said.
    "Dig right here," he said [!!!].
    And he dug a trench, Golizhi did.

        -2-
(42) After he dug a ditch, he built a fire.
    He put the food into the pit.
    Then he [Ma'i] thought of something new.

        -1-
(43) "Let's have a foot race, shiłna'ash.
    Whoever comes back first,
        this will be his," he said.   *light laughter*
    "No," he [Golizhi] said, but he [Ma'i] won the argument.
    "I can't run fast," he [Golizhi] said.
    "While I stay here, you start loping," he [Ma'i] said.

        -1-
(44) . . . [indistinct] . . . while Ma'i pretended to do something
        to his ankles, he [Golizhi] started to run,
    then, over the hill he ran,
        and ran into an abandoned hole.

        -2-
(45) In a little while, he [Ma'i] suddenly spurted away.

        -3-
(46) A torch he tied to his tail
    and the smoke was pouring out behind him
        as he ran.   *[laughter]*

	-17-	*laughter*

G (47) While he was running over there,
    Golizhi ran back, it is said,
        there where he had buried the food [!!!].
    He dug them up and took them up into the rocks,
        it is said.   *amusement*
    Four little prairie dogs he reburied,
    then he was sitting back up there, it is said.
    [!!!] Ma'i ran back, it is said,   *light laughter*
        back to the place where the prairie dogs were buried.
    He leaped over it.   [*laughter*]

                -4-   *increased laughter*

(48) "Hwah!" he said.   [*laughter*]

                -8-   *extended laughter*

(49) "Shiłna'ash—I wonder how far back he's plodding,
        Mr. His-Urine," he said.

                -6-   *loud laughter*

(50) [!!!] Sighing, he lay down,
        pretended to lie down, in the shade.
    He jumped up and leaped over to the pit.   [*laughter*]

                -1-   *laughter*

(51) He thrust a pointed object into the ground
        and grabbed the tail of the prairie dog first, it is said.
    Only the tail came loose.   [*chuckle*]

                -1-   *light laughter*

(52) "Oh no! the fire has gotten to the tail," he said.

                -2-   *loud laughter*

(53) So he grabbed the stick and thrust it into the ground again;
        a little prairie dog he dug up, it is said.
    "I'm not going to eat this [meat]," he said,
        and he flung it away toward the east.

                -2-   *light laughter*

(54) He thrust it into the ground again;   [*slower*]
        a little prairie dog he dug up.
    "I'm not going to eat this," he said,
        and he flung it away toward the south.

                -2-   *light laughter*

(55) He thrust it into the ground again;   [*slower*]
        a little prairie dog he dug up.

"I'm not going to eat this," he said,
    and he flung it away toward the west.

-2- *breathing*

(56) He thrust it into the ground again; [*sleepily*]
    a little prairie dog he dug up.
"I'm not going to eat this," he said,
    and he flung it away toward the north.

-1- *breathing*

(57) He thrust repeatedly in many places, it is said,
    and couldn't find any.
Nothing, it is said.
There weren't any, it is said.

-2- *expelling breath*

(58) He couldn't, he walked [frustrated] around in circles.
He went around and he picked up those little prairie dogs he had
    thrown away.
Then he picked up every little bit
    and ate it all.

-2- *quiet laughter*

H (59) Then he started to follow [Golizhi's] tracks, it is said, *amusement*
    but he couldn't pick up the trail.
He kept following the tracks, back and forth,
    to where the rock meets the sand. *boy: hn!*
(He didn't bother to look up.)

-2-

(60) He [Golizhi] dropped a bone and he [Ma'i] looked up, it is said.
It dropped at his feet.

-1- *quiet laughter*

(61) "Shiłna'ash, share with me again
[implied: what I shared with you previously]." [*brief laughter*]

-5- *brief laughter*

(62) "Certainly not," he said to him, it is said. [*slowly, seriously*]
He was begging, to no avail, it is said.
Golizhi kept dropping bones down to him.
He chewed the bones, it is said.

-4- *small burst of quiet laughter*

I (63) That's how it happened, it is said.

Comments, Notes, Comparisons

For the cultural "meaning" and function of the story, see the text and notes of the prose version. Following are some particular ideas that have come forth from the new translation. Many of these matters are implied or rationalized in the explanations for the prose text, but here they have had to be dealt with head-on. Where considerable discrepancies (real or apparent) exist between the two versions, some accounting is given for the difference.

Several stylistic elements are found throughout. For one thing, pronouns referring to Ma'i and Golizhi are those normally used in reference to human persons, not animals. Similarly, reference to body parts is often in the form of human anatomy, as in verse 11, where "toes" does not denote animal paws. Again, in verse 28, "people" or "folks" is the best rendering of the collective term for the dancing animals — not the term one would normally use to denote something like a herd or pack or troop of animals. All of these suggest little differentiation between humans and animals in the Ma'i stories, for several reasons. For one thing, the story is framed in a mythic dimension in which all possibilities are inherent, and thus factual division on physiological, biological bases (which the Navajos are keenly aware of and articulate about) is pointless. Also, as noted in the earlier article, these stories are told more to suggest a set of ethics for humans than to provide an explanation for, or exposition of, animal physiology and behavior. Referring to animals in human terms perhaps makes the abstract connections more realizable.

Another important stylistic element is Yellowman's use of a nasal, slow delivery for Ma'i's speech. The marginal notes indicate lines in which this is particularly marked, but it is necessary to remember that the style is used throughout. It is widely found in the narration of Coyote tales, and listeners look forward to its familiar tone, which is considered distinctive to the genre. So pleasant and humorous are its effects on auditors that Coyote tales without it are almost unthinkable; its presence is one dimension of the "pretty languages," the special vocabulary of beautiful ideas and textures which, in the Navajo view, are reflections of stability and order in the world (quite in contradistinction to the unstable actions of Coyote, for whose odd personality this textural network of sound acts as an ironic counterpoint).

The central actions in each scene are noticeably energetic: trotting, running, dancing, jumping, throwing. It is worth recalling that movement itself is central to Navajo thought, language, and world view. Movement is the normal condition of life. One way to intensify this idea, of course, is to accelerate it, to keep the pace worked up. It is only late in the story, after Ma'i has leaped over the cooking pit so arrogantly and has so foolishly thrown away his food, that the pace slackens to something "normal." The final scene, a tableau in which the would-be manipulator must beg for scraps from someone above him, is the only scene in which rapid movement does not take place. The pace of moral discovery and comeuppance is that of everyday life. Aggression, competition, selfishness, arrogance are out of proportion to regular movement.

Scene A

The opening is formulaic, standardized. It suggests both a particular place in Navajo country and a concept of continuity and movement in mythic reality. Ma'i has always been in motion and always will be. The phrasing suggests that we, in our present time frame, are breaking into something that has been happening continuously from out of the past, something like opening a play or a movie *in medias res:* "As we join the story we find . . ." We are looking through a narrative window, so to speak, at another dimension of life in which actions are always in progress. Further, the term *joldloshi* is used only of Ma'i in the Coyote tales. Normally, an animal trotting would be described as *yildlosh;* here the *jol* is distinctive of Ma'i's mythic trotting—which is always pregnant with meaning—and the suffix-*i* implies recklessness, abandon. The first line, then, *Ma'i joldloshi lá eeyá,* in which *lá* suggests past action and *eeyá* suggests the present, encapsulates a rich and complicated set of postulates within which the rest of the story has expanded meaning.

The original translation mentions a once forested area, inferred from the desert setting and the depiction of wood floating away. This is probably unwarranted, after all; at least it is irrelevant.

Scene B

Both the "I wish" of the prose translation and the "If it would only" of the poetic rendering are awkward and superficially simple-sounding attempts to represent the Navajo subjunctive, in which speaking about something is a way of projecting its real possibility. It relates to much of ritual language, in which the condition of the patient is spoken about and chanted over, in which a stable world of *reality* is created through the use of key words. Thus, whereas the subjunctive in European languages has the connotation of wishful thinking or even make-believe, in Navajo it has the feel of creation. In the case of Ma'i, moreover, the audience knows from other mythic stories that control of the rains was given to him in earlier negotiations with the Holy Persons. His speaking of rain thus starts the story on a note of natural response and fertility, certainly an ironic setting against which to view his angry and selfish move toward impoverishment and hunger.

The thirteen-second pause between verses 14 and 15 was not rhetorical but circumstantial. A baby held by Yellowman wet its diapers (and Yellowman's leg), began to cry, and was handed over to its mother.

Scene C

Some serious discrepancies between translations can be seen in the interchange between Ma'i and Golizhi (verse 18). "Skunk didn't know he was there" and "Skunk turned around in fright" are simply not in the original narration and may have been inserted in the earlier translation as ways of making the scene more palpable to English readers. Further, Ma'i does not call to Golizhi four times; apparently Toelken mistook a sound in the term *bididį́į́nil* ("you tell them") for *dį́į́'* ("four"). "Skunk had a dipper" is not specifically stated in translatable form, but the idea is clearly to be inferred, since the Navajo term for fetching water is not the same as for simply going to the water to drink it there (note also the human aspect of bringing water home). Obviously, a container is involved.

Scenes C and D

Verses 20–26 and 27 reveal the original narration of Ma'i's plan and Golizhi's willing application of it. The prose translation expanded on the meaning of the plan and reported it as repeated in essence by Golizhi in the small animals' village. Actually, while the details seem parsimonious in the new direct translation, the scene is far richer than it may first appear. Ma'i here talks about himself in the third person, as if to embody others' views of him; when Golizhi transmits this statement to the prairie dogs, we are told he "gave out the word," which in Navajo is something like bringing all the news. That is, we are to assume that Golizhi's disclosure is a complete recapitulation of those details outlined by Ma'i as a way of deceiving the small animals. This is now followed by an extended use of "It's true!" along with attempts by the animals to verify Ma'i's death, not only providing the irony that deception is going undetected in the midst of declarations of truth but suggesting now that their own blindness may be involved in the animals' demise.

Scene E

In verse 33 the dance is described very distinctly in Navajo: its direction is circular; the dancers are moving around in unison in surges or waves; and the couples joining are stepping in at these periodic moments of movement. The regularity, the periodicity, the circularity are all aspects of beauty, *hózhǫ́:* they are some of the cultural referents of what Helen Yellowman called "those pretty languages."

The suffix *-ye-ne* on Golizhi's name in verse 35 means that the person so called is dead, or cursed. Here it indicates the narrator's dislike for him (or at least for the role he plays here in deception). In verse 35, Golizhi rehearses to himself the specific directions given to him previously by Ma'i; thus "he" in the last line obviously refers to Ma'i.

In verse 36, Golizhi clearly calls the prairie dogs' attention to the bird (whose name here might mean "white under the wings while overhead") only once, not four times as given in the first translation. Apparently Toelken misheard *déé'* ("from") for *dį́į'* ("four").

In verse 38, Ma'i jumps up and pretends (?) anger that the prairie dogs should call him dead. In English it might read, "Oh, so you say I'm dead, do you?" or " 'The hated one is dead,' is he?"

Scene F

Note the dropping of proper names to a minimum during the cooking and race scenes. The audience knows very well who is who, and the pronoun "he" does not here produce confusion.

In verse 43, instead of "Ma'i insisted" — as in the prose translation — note that he simply uses the tactic of going ahead with his plan regardless of Golizhi's objections. The effect is the same, but as is the case with most of this story, the event should be perceived as action, not as indirect description of attitude.

The rather long pause after verse 46 is no doubt due to some conversation that arose among the visitors. It was quiet and unobtrusive (and the visitors could not understand the story narration anyhow), but it probably constituted a brief distraction. On the tape the narration continues about four seconds after the conversation dies down.

Ma'i's rapid return to the cooking pit (verse 47) is described in the prose translation as an attempt to "make a good finish." This is partly supported by the [!!!] that precedes the utterance; more obvious is the fact that instead of stopping, under control, Ma'i leaps right over the spot. It's overacted, in other words; Scott calls it "obvious arrogance."

Scene G

After Ma'i's return run he rests briefly, then leaps over to the cooking pit. Tying this in with "pretended to lie down" and his later pacing back and forth,

Toelken earlier understood the movement as an attempt to show how long he had waited for Golizhi before impatiently digging up the cooked prairie dogs. Scott feels rather that the present translation justifies a stress only on Ma'i's impatience and selfishness. He makes little pretense at waiting but jumps directly toward what he thinks will be a banquet. Although he has won (he thinks) and can therefore claim the prairie dogs, Navajo custom would have him distribute shares to those who are in subordinate or associate status.

Verses 53–56 show the actual wording of the exhumation scene. One by one, in nearly exact repetition, Ma'i digs up the prairie dogs and flings them toward the cardinal directions *in ritual order,* starting in the east and continuing in a "sunwise" direction just as Navajo ceremonial movements are organized. Since his intent is selfish and his actions wasteful, however, this constitutes at least a perversion of ritual, a desecration of sacred order by subordinating it to personal appetites. The original translation reduces the redundancy by collapsing these important actions too far.

A similar reduction of meaning is found in the passage represented by verse 57: the prose translation gives no sense of the repeated or intensified negative results of Ma'i's digging in various places. It is important because of its relation to Ma'i's frustration in the next verse (58), the sense of which is totally missing from the earlier text. Yellowman does not stumble here; he intentionally words the line "He couldn't, he walked around," so as to express the way in which Ma'i's walking is a measure of his inability to find what he "knows" is there. Instead of saying, "Ma'i was frustrated," Yellowman narrates a scene of frustration, using phrasing that suggests a mental impasse.

Conclusions

The use of *hááhgóóshį́į́* ([!!!]), totally missed in the first translation, begs for comment but defies full analysis. Clearly it is used in very important passages (but not in every key passage, it would seem). In six instances it appears in lines that concern large gatherings of animals (B3, B4, D28 [twice], E33, E34); the open area as setting is stressed (B3); in D27 and E34 the lie that "the hated one is washed out," is spoken, first by Golizhi, then by the crowd; Ma'i's instructions to Golizhi about the deceptive dance are stressed (E35); Ma'i's sudden "resurrection" and use of his clubs are foregrounded (E38, E39); Ma'i's ordering Golizhi to dig in a particular spot is stressed (F41), as is the return of both animals from the race (G47); finally, Ma'i's pretended wait (G50) is underlined. Are these key elements of cultural reference, foregrounded for some special reason? Are they simply aspects of Yellowman's presentation, allowing for the building of particularly vivid or intensified scenes (other scenes being intensified by still other devices such as pacing, intonation, ritual inferences, and so on)? The latter is more likely the case, but a demonstration of it would require an equally detailed look at several other stories told by the same narrator *and* a survey of other orally delivered stories by other Navajo raconteurs. We have decided to be prudent and not try to eat all the prairie dogs at once.

One final comment on meaning seems appropriate after all the detail of this scrutiny. In the original article, Toelken held that the real cultural meaning of the tale resided not in its structure but in its texture. This was stated so baldly for two reasons: first, accounting for the details of plot structure seemed to elucidate so few of those elements which were clearly of importance to the Navajos, and seemed in fact to do no more than solidify the stereotype of Indian literature as childlike, simple, uncomplicated (read: unworthy of notice by serious scholars of "real" literature); second, it was meant as a direct statement to those who were at the time classifying and studying nearly everything in folklore in structural terms (usually *lineal* terms, at that, which covertly—and murderously—subordinate all traditional materials to the Western world view: classification, analysis, and evaluation). Toelken hoped to show that the quarry was "in another place." But as bald tactical pronouncements often turn out, this one was oversimplified, for the "meaning," really, is no more *in* the texture than it is *in* the structure. Actually, structure and texture unite to provide an excitement of meaning which already exists elsewhere, in the shared ideas and customs of people raised in an intensely traditional society. The structure provides the framework of something recognizable taking place through a brief span of time. The texture evokes emotional and philosophical attitudes, moral assessments, and ethical responses by bringing certain performance features together in such a way as to create models of, and challenges to, recognizable clusters of belief.[56] But these beliefs, attitudes, responses, and so on, are the results of long years of traditional development, experience, ritual practice, human evaluations of old ideas as they are seen in continually changing historical contexts. Thus, the stories act like "surface structure" in language: by their articulation they touch off a Navajo's deeper accumulated sense of reality; they excite perspectives on truth by bringing together a "critical mass" made up of ethical opposites (one thinks of the Zen *koan* here); they provide culturally enjoyable correlatives to a body of thought so complicated and profound that vicarious experience in it through entertainment is one of the only access points available to most people.[57]

We overheard a literature professor say that if only every other chapter had been deleted from *Moby Dick,* Melville might have made a decent whaling story out of it. We hope it is clear from the evidence brought forward here that the same effect may be had in Native American literature by simply presenting the text in prose and by ignoring those textural references that make it as impossible for a listener to think a story is "about an adventure of a coyote" as it is for a reader of Melville, no matter how dull, to think that *Moby Dick* is "a story about a whale."

Notes

1. See Dell H. Hymes, "Discovering Oral Performance and Measured Verse in American Indian Narrative," *New Literary History* 8 (spring 1977): 433–57; Hymes, "Breakthrough into Performance," in *Folklore: Performance and Communication,* ed. Dan Ben-Amos and Kenneth S. Goldstein (The Hague: Mouton, 1975), pp. 11–74; Hymes, "Folklore's Nature and the Sun's Myth," *Journal of American Folklore* 88, no. 4 (1975): 345–69; Dennis Tedlock, *Finding the Center: Narrative Poetry of the Zuni Indians* (New York: Dial, 1972; rpt. Lincoln: University of Nebraska Press, 1978); Tedlock, "On the Translation of Style in Oral Narrative," in *Toward New Perspectives in Folklore,* ed. Américo Paredes and Richard Bauman (Austin: University of Texas Press, 1971), pp. 114–33.

2. The Sun's Myth may be found in Franz Boas, *Kathlamet Texts,* Bureau of American Ethnology Bulletin no. 26 (Washington DC: GPO, 1901), pp. 26–33.

3. Prose translation and interlinear text in Franz Boas, *Tsimshian Texts,* Bureau of American Ethnology Bulletin no. 27 (Washington DC: GPO, 1902), pp. 200–210; the first passage is on p. 203, the second on pp. 209–10.

4. Barre Toelken, "The 'Pretty Languages' of Yellowman: Genre, Mode, and Texture in Navajo Coyote Narratives," *Genre* 2 (September 1969): 311–35; rpt. in *Folklore Genres,* ed. Dan Ben-Amos (Austin: University of Texas Press, 1976), pp. 145–70. This article was an expansion of a paper presented at the 1967 annual meeting of the American Folklore Society at Toronto. Travel grants to support recording and further study were provided by the Department of English and by the Office of Scientific and Scholarly Research of the University of Oregon. For supplying first aid to the author's failing Navajo language and for providing excellent comments on the nature of this investigation, I remain deeply indebted to Annie and Helen Yellowman, daughters of the narrator, and to the Reverend Canon H. B. Liebler, longtime Episcopal missionary to the Navajos.

5. By way of only a few examples, see Gladys Reichard, *Navaho Religion* (New York: Pantheon, 1950), concordance A; Leland C. Wyman, ed., *Beautyway: A Navaho Ceremonial* (New York: Bollinger Foundation, 1957), p. 131; Wyman, *The Red Antway of the Navaho,* Navaho Religion Series, vol. 5 (Santa Fe NM: Museum of Navajo Ceremonial Art, 1965);

David P. McAllester, ed., *The Myth and Prayers of the Great Star Chant, and the Myth of the Coyote Chant,* Navaho Religion Series, vol. 4 (Santa Fe NM: Museum of Navajo Ceremonial Art, 1956), pp. 91–105; Father Berard Haile, O.F.M., and Mary C. Wheelwright, eds., *Emergence Myth,* Navaho Religion Series, vol. 3 (Santa Fe NM: Museum of Navajo Ceremonial Art, 1949), p. 130.

6. See note 11, below, concerning Sapir's text of the tale used in this study. Note that the proper spelling of the term is *jiní;* the proper translation is "it is said."

7. Perhaps it is well to explain that this adoption featured none of the Hollywood elements that might be imagined by the reader who is unfamiliar with the Navajos. Tsinaabąąs Yazhi simply announced at an evening meal that he was going to be my father and that henceforth I was probably to be known to others as Tsinaabąąs Yazhi Biyé' (Little Wagon's Son). After that point my address to him was *shizhé'é* ("my father") instead of the joking *shicheii* ("my grandfather"); my form of address to his daughter, therefore, became *shádí* ("my older sister"), and to her husband, Yellowman, *shiłna'ash* [the ł here is pronounced like the Welsh *ll;* that is, a voiceless lateral fricative] (lit. "one who walks with me," used with the sense of "my kinsman," "my cousin").

8. His comments have been augmented by those of his daughters, one of whom supplied my title during a session in which Yellowman attempted to explain his choice of vocabulary in the Coyote tales. I was having difficulty with a certain phrase when Helen Yellowman interjected in English, "He just means he uses those pretty languages."

9. Melville Jacobs made this observation in his extremely valuable study, *The Content and Style of an Oral Literature: Clackamas Chinook Texts,* Viking Publications in Anthropology 26 (Chicago: University of Chicago Press, 1959), p. 128. But even Jacobs's title betrays the fact that our culture makes a distinction between sacred and secular which is not so clearly marked in most Indian tribes (and particularly the Navajo).

10. David F. Aberle, *The Peyote Religion among the Navaho* (Chicago: University of Chicago Press, 1966), p. 103 n. Aberle notes that some people did respond to only one question, which may mean the custom is breaking down. It is difficult to determine, however, how even the occasional recourse to this custom may affect data drawn from questionnaires as they are subjected to statistical analysis.

11. Elsie Clews Parsons presented a text of it with the title "Coyote Plays Dead," in "Navaho Folk Tales," *Journal of American Folklore* 36, no. 2 (1923): 371–72, and related it to a Pueblo tale of suspected Spanish origin, which appeared in her earlier article, "Pueblo-Indian Folk-Tales, Probably of Spanish Provenience," *Journal of American Folklore* 31, no. 2 (1918): 229–30. A very awkward native text titled "Coyote Makes Rain" is given in Edward Sapir and Harry Hoijer, eds., *Navaho Texts* (Iowa City, Iowa: Linguistic Society of America, 1942), pp. 20–25; it employs the self-conscious *jiní* ("it is said") thirty-nine times in what appears to me a much collapsed form of the story.

12. The Navajo wording here is complex and refers to this story as one of a series of

repeated actions. The closest English equivalent that I can think of would be "in one of these episodes," but I have avoided that translation because it implies something more objectively literary than does the original. The point, however, is more than linguistic: Yellowman here limits himself to one incident in Coyote's career but opens the narration in such a way as to remind his listeners of the whole fabric of Coyote legend. Compare the presumable effect of this on native listeners with that of Sapir's text (note 11), where the narrator is telling a tale to an outsider, in which the first phrase translates, "Long ago Coyote was trotting along, they say."

13. Ma'i does not want to alert the prairie dogs, but in order to get the desired results he must speak these wishes aloud. Therefore, he phrases them as if he were seeking only personal respite from the heat (Yellowman).

14. The word Yellowman uses here would normally be translated "palms"; it is one of several indications throughout the Coyote canon (and supported by Yellowman in conversation) that Coyote is not always envisioned as a coyote.

15. *Golizhi,* lit. "one whose urine stinks."

16. I retain this term for lack of a proper English equivalent, and because it is distinctive to the speech of Coyote. Meaning literally "one who walks with me," it is used familiarly among male friends in the figurative sense of "cousin," or even something like the English "old buddy." Essentially, it is a term of trust as well as friendship or relation. Coyote uses the term constantly, especially when he is trying to put something over on someone else; thus its appearance usually creates a sense of irony, and its retention here may help signal its literary function for the English reader. As indicated above (note 7), the *l* is pronounced as a voiceless lateral fricative.

17. Four is the number in Navajo narrative, custom, and ritual which corresponds to three in European-American folklore. Usually the fourth position "carries the weight," and normally the narrator works up to the fourth, utilizing (as we do in "Cinderella" or "The Three Pigs") the audience's recognition of the sequence to build tension. Here, however, Yellowman condenses the sequence with this descriptive comment. It seems to me that a possible aesthetic explanation might be that the humor (as the laughter suggests) has been chiefly connected to the first position; the rest, being important but anticlimactic, is telescoped. I have neglected to consult Yellowman on the matter, however.

18. Lit., "slender grass," a certain variety of desert grass the heads of which look like small, twisted green worms. I have not been able to find a botanical name for it.

19. The phrase uses *hatal,* "sing," which usually implies a ceremony connected with healing or purifying.

20. In this discussion of "what is true" there is a predominance of the vowel sound *aa,* with and without nasalization. The textural ramifications of this feature are discussed below. See also notes 25 and 27 for similar passages.

21. Annie Yellowman: "It's a special kind of bird."

22. Lit., "urine."

23. Annie Y.: Now he can have revenge because their previous insults have been made even more serious by this false claim that he is dead.

24. As usual, Ma'i cons someone else into doing the work.

25. There is heavy use of *qq* throughout the description of Skunk hiding and Ma'i running past; see also notes 20 and 27.

26. Yellowman: He ties the burning stick to his tail in order to show off how fast he can run. Readers familiar with Navajo lore will recognize in this scene an important motif in the story of Coyote's theft of fire.

27. There is heavy use of *qq* in the exhumation scene; see notes 20 and 25.

28. Probably to avoid being burned; Ma'i avoids discomfort.

29. This is humorous in part because he has already covered the ground with his own footprints: the mark of a poor hunter, and thus subject to ridicule.

30. Emphatic: *dooda hee.*

31. This is Yellowman's favorite ending formula. In my references to the narrator's change of tones and styles, I have included only those variations of importance to the present study. The reader will note that most of the highly nasalized passages occur in the speech of characters; it can be assumed here that passages which are not marked were delivered in a regular narrative tone, which for Yellowman's rendition of the Coyote stories is slightly more nasalized than normal conversation and somewhat more slowly delivered.

32. This is not a new idea, of course. Hennigh puts it in a succinct cross-cultural context which nicely demonstrates the central point. See Lawrence Hennigh, "Control of Incest in Eskimo Folktales," *Journal of American Folklore* 79, no. 2 (1966): 356–69.

33. Father Liebler, called "priest with long hair" by the Navajos, was the founder, builder, and vicar of St. Christopher's Mission to the Navajo at Bluff, Utah. In "retirement," he and a small group of faithful retainers built the Hat Rock Valley Retreat Center, near Oljeto. His "Christian Concepts and Navaho Words," *Utah Humanities Review* 13, no. 1 (1959): 169–75; and "The Social and Cultural Patterns of the Navajo Indians," *Utah Historical Quarterly* 30, no. 4 (1962): 299–325, illustrate his familiarity with Navajo language and culture.

34. Reichard, *Navaho Religion,* p. 267, points out that such language may not actually be archaic; its special usage sets it apart, and its users might attribute its effects to archaism, but it is still in wide use and is understood by all native speakers, including children.

35. This is a literal translation of the idiom; it may also mean, "They make things simple, or easy to understand."

36. Reichard, *Navaho Religion,* has a good discussion of Navajo symbolism. My own acquaintance with the symbols themselves, especially in relation to particular rituals, is spotty enough to prevent a full evaluation of Reichard's comments, but I can say that her willingness to allow for conscious art seems quite sensible; see especially her discussion of the Navajo awareness of word as symbol (p. 267).

37. Clyde Kluckhohn and Dorothea Leighton, *The Navaho,* rev. ed. (Garden City NY: Doubleday, 1962), p. 194.

38. W. W. Hill, *Navaho Humor,* General Series in Anthropology 9 (Menasha, Wis., 1943), p. 19.

39. Alan Dundes, "Texture, Text, and Context," *Southern Folklore Quarterly* 28, no. 4 (1964): 251–65.

40. By structure I mean the formal framework, the lineal or organized form of a traditional text. In narrative, it is that particular sequence of events which makes up the story line and plot; structure is, then, the rational design of the story. Although in actual artistic practice, texture and structure are tightly interrelated, one can separate for purposes of discussion what is being said from how it is being said. It is usually on the basis of structure that definitions of genre are founded in literature.

41. Dundes, "Texture, Text, and Context," p. 254.

42. René Wellek and Austin Warren, *Theory of Literature* (New York: Harcourt, Brace, 1942), pp. 235, 241, for example.

43. Northrop Frye, *Anatomy of Criticism* (New York: Atheneum, 1967), pp. 246–48.

44. Jacobs has suggested (*Content and Style,* pp. 211–19) that our conceptions of drama much more closely match the characteristics of folk "stories," for in most cases (at least in most Indian materials) a tale is not told in its entirety; rather, certain key features and actions are described in such a way as to cause the audience to envision a drama in progress. The audience creates a mental stage upon which characters manipulated by the narrator play their scenes. I suspect that this may be true of all oral "narrative," including such things as the ballads and tales of our own culture, and that our penchant for applying generic terms based on visible form to oral materials has led us constantly away from the essence we seek.

45. See notes 20, 25, and 27, above.

46. See Reichard, *Navaho Religion,* p. 90.

47. Hill, *Navaho Humor,* p. 23.

48. Hill, *Navaho Humor,* p. 21.

49. Hennigh, "Control of Incest," p. 368.

50. On order and Navajo ritual, see Reichard, *Navaho Religion,* pp. 183, 80–81; in the remainder of this discussion it is important to keep in mind that culturally the Navajos are "nomadic," that their whole view of life seems based on a sense of where they stand in relation to a changing landscape. As Hoijer has pointed out, this characteristic is reflected deeply by the Navajo language, which defines position by withdrawal of motion, has very few nouns, and most often uses substantives that are actually descriptions of movements: *haniibąąz,* lit. "a hoop-like object has rolled out," means "full moon." See Harry Hoijer, "Cultural Implications of Some Navaho Linguistic Categories," in *Language in Culture and Society,* ed. Dell H. Hymes (New York: Harper & Row, 1964), pp. 142–48.

51. Reichard, *Navaho Religion,* p. 5.

52. Hill, *Navaho Humor,* p. 23.

53. Reichard, *Navaho Religion,* p. 119.

54. Reichard, *Navaho Religion,* pp. 422–26.

55. Hymes, "Discovering Oral Performance," pp. 453–54.

56. We are much indebted to Dell Hymes for helping to clarify this matter in personal correspondence. Besides having dedicated a large part of his life to translating and understanding Native American literature, he has unselfishly urged on and encouraged many of those now seriously engaged in this field. His personal and scholarly generosity are in large part responsible for the current standing of this profession.

57. To move from this level of discourse to a deeper awareness of how these stories fit into Navajo culture and world view, one must at least consult Gary Witherspoon's tour de force, *Language and Art in the Navajo Universe* (Ann Arbor: University of Michigan Press, 1977); it treats such subjects as creativity through language, order and harmony, and other matters brought up in this article by showing how they grow out of and relate to Navajo language. Among other things, Witherspoon notes that there are only a few conjugations of the verb "to be" but 356,200 distinct conjugations for the verb "to go," giving statistical support to the well-known concept put forward by nearly every specialist on the Navajos that the Navajo world view is far more interested in movement than in physical stasis. This work should now be obligatory for anyone wishing to see Navajo culture more fully.

If Texts Are Prayers,
What Do Wintus Want?

LINDA AINSWORTH

As early as 1939, Kenneth Burke criticized Freud and psychoanalytic theory for its too static model of literary interpretation. According to Burke, psychoanalysis overlooked the fact that a text can be a "prayer," not just the manifestation of wish fulfillment.[1] As "prayers," texts constitute rhetorical gestures that take at least part of their meaning from the ends they wish to bring about. These ends may be purely affective ones, requiring something as seemingly innocuous as an emotional response, or they may require some action on the part of the audience. In either case, the purpose of the text is to bring about some change in the way the audience acts or feels about some issue or issues. What bothered Burke most about the Freudian psychoanalytic model was that it was too eager to accept the text as a manifestation of the *fulfilled* desires of the speaker and the audience, no matter how well mediated the symbolic language.

We might well argue that Freud neither intended nor would have endorsed such a reductionist application of psychoanalytic theory. Nevertheless, such thinking prevails in much psychoanalytic interpretation of texts, especially those from so-called alien or exotic cultures. It abounds, for example, in functionalist interpretations of traditional narrative art. Many of these interpretations suggest that texts dealing with subjects such as incest exist to reinforce taboos about incest; that is, texts exist to augment prevailing cultural practices.

More recent readings of Freud, as well as the resurgence of interest in object relations theories, have led to the introduction of new psychoanalytic models that allow for much richer interpretations of literary texts, even ones we are least familiar (and least comfortable) with, including those from the oral Native American tradition. One such model, derived primarily from object relations theory, focuses our attention on the rhetorical features of the text and demands that we consider not only what the text seems to represent but also why such a representation is necessary at all if cultural consensus prevails regarding a particular practice. It also asks us to consider the quality and nature of the text's appeal and to whom it might appeal. It is a model, in other words, that allows for an examination of the culture-making processes that go into the creation of certain texts and not just the itemization of the cultural practices manifest in a text.[2]

Object relations theory retreats from Freudian theory in its emphasis on pre-oedipal stages of development. It centers on the relationship between infant and mother, not oedipal child and father, and argues that the primary object of concern in character formation is the breast and not the phallus. Both Melanie Klein and Donald Winnicott stress the importance of the weaning stages to the attachments infants form to "transitional objects," objects essential to the development and maintenance of the cultural symbols that constitute, through their contiguity with other cultural practices, the boundaries between cultures. In the words of Peter Brooks, Klein argues that "the mother's body, especially the breast, provides the original object of symbolization, and then the field of exploration" for what Brooks terms the "epistemophilic impulse," or the urge to know.[3] Part of what the child wants to know, according to Klein, is where she stands in relation to the absence of the primary object and the introduction of secondary objects. What is made manifest throughout the weaning process is that the child engages in sadistic fantasies designed to transform his anger and anxiety at the loss of the breast into a rejection of the breast and a preference for substitute objects.

Winnicott turns his attention to the importance of transitional objects in the development of play. He argues that "the place where cultural experience is located is in the potential space between the individual and the environment (originally the object [i.e., the breast]). The same can be said of playing. Cultural experience begins with creative living first manifested in play."[4] All creative life results from the accommodations the child makes in relation to the once present, then absent, breast and the objects she adapts to forestall feelings of loss. Winnicott stresses the term *potential* space, because it is in all instances a hypothetical space full of paradoxes. It exists as space to be repudiated and filled with transitional objects. Though symbolically nullified as soon as manifest, its presence is essential to the development of the cultural life of the child, and the transitional objects that succeed in diverting attention from the primary object form the basis for the symbolic ideation that "feeds" the cultural experience. The exact contours and qualities of this potential space can be known not in generalized terms but only through close examination of the relationship between any one baby and his mother. Generalizing statements about its contour or quality must be stated in the idiom of the culture itself and at best can be only proximate.

Both Klein and Winnicott emphasize what is lost in the culture-making process all individuals engage in. Burke, too, in his insistence on the text as "prayer," focuses our attention on what the text attempts to bring into existence, that something which is absent in the culture as it stands. No matter how fervently we defend cultural practice and no matter how eloquently we articulate its many subtleties, we must nevertheless recognize that the symbols that encode cultural practice are but flimsy substitutes for the objects we, even in maturity, still long for. What seems most important is the way in which texts, when considered as elaborate and sophisticated transitional objects, mediate to fill the space between what we have and what we have not. In other words, texts are very much about consolation prizes, about accommodations we make in lieu of having what we want.

That recognition is essential to understanding the complexity and richness of the cultural symbols found in such a story as "Talimlɛluhɛrɛs and Rolling Head Loon Woman." [5] In this tale, cultural taboos related to the onset of menses and the expression of inappropriate incestuous feelings fail to defend a family against the all-consuming oral aggressiveness of a young daughter. Giving rein to such feelings, no matter how innocently she does so, the pubescent girl brings about the destruction of the family.

Talimlɛluhɛrɛs and Rolling Head Loon Woman

Long ago there came into being some people who had four children, two boys and two girls, and who owned a big earth lodge. The adolescent boy stayed in the earth lodge always. In the meantime his younger sister reached adolescence. So they left her in the menstrual hut for some nights. Now his younger sister loved him who was in the earth lodge, Talimlɛluhɛrɛs. So she went to him, got into bed with him, tickled him and sat all over him. However her elder brother said, "What is the matter with you, younger sister?" and she left. So she came to him, sometimes in the evening, sometimes in the early morning, and she bothered him as before, tickling him. And as before he said, "What is the matter with you, younger sister?" So at last her elder brother told his sister, "Elder sister, here to me, all the time to me, comes to me my younger sister," he said. And his sister went to her younger sister and asked, "Why do you always bother my younger brother?" And the other said, "I never bother him." Then the other said, "Younger sister, go get maple. Make yourself a front apron." So she went to get it, climbed around on the maple trees and peeled, kept on peeling, and cut her finger. And for a while she stood there with blood dripping to the ground. Then she sucked the blood. She did not know what to do, so she sucked it in and spat it out, and as she did so the blood tasted sweet to her, so now, first because she wanted to swallow blood and then because she wanted to eat her flesh, she devoured her flesh and turned into a

Rolling Head (*K'opk'opmas*). All around the world she went, devouring people. She left for herself only her elder sister, her younger brother, and her elder brother.

Now they were afraid and started to climb up above. They heard her below going about wildly everywhere asking everything, the rock beings, the tree beings, asking all. And they said, "We don't know." They added, "You grew into something else and yet you know nothing." So she asked some ancient faeces and they said, "You grew into something else and yet you know nothing. Look up above." So she looked up and saw them going halfway up. So she jumped up, and grabbed, and pulled down, and then lay on her back, and spread her legs. He who was going above, her elder brother, fell between her thighs. She was very excited.

And the rest went above empty-handed. "Oh, dear, our own child has orphaned us," said the old man. They cried. And the older daughter said, "However long it may take, I'll find my younger brother." So they went up above.

Now her elder brother would have nothing to do with her, and turned on his side. So, in one lick as it were, she devoured him, his heart alone she hung around her neck and went toward the north drainage, alighted with it on a big lake, swam about with it, stayed there with it. Every evening at sunset she came, skimming the water, to a large sandy beach on the east shore, south, south to the sandy beach, on the south she alighted and stayed.

The people wanted to catch her but did not know how. Humming-Bird said, "Let me go," he said, "let me watch." The people said, "Yes," and he said to the elder sister, "Make a good cooking basket," he said. "Then have on hand white rocks, good ones which will hold heat," he said. He did not come, and did not come, and then finally he arrived. He arrived and told them, "I saw her," he said. "She has a heart hung around her neck. At sunset she alights on the sand on the south beach. From the north she comes." And the people said, "Let's go and watch," they said. Then they said to the little boy, "You go and watch," they said. They gave him a good sharp untipped arrow. "When you see her, pierce her, and when you pierce her she'll go south, she'll get out and make a bee-line, and go south to the sand beach." To the woman they said, "You go and sit on the south bank, on the sandy beach. Have the cooking basket half full of water and heat the white rocks well and drop them in. And when he pierces her go quickly, get her, grab her, and slip the heart off over her head. Put it into the cooking basket and cover it up quickly."

At sunset they were there. And the elder sister sat on the south bank on the beach, as she had already been directed. She went there and watched. As she watched at sunset the water was heard roaring in the north. She did not come, and then, at last, she saw her come and get out on the south bank, and behold, she had been pierced by the untipped arrow. She went quickly and slipped off the heart and put it into the cooking basket. Then she took it home. "This is my younger brother's heart," she said. So they steamed it, and while they were steaming it, it came to life, but though he was a person he did not look right. He did not live very long.

Even a cursory reading of this story reveals a number of universal clichés about the female body and the threat to social integrity posed by expressions of female sexual desire. Moreover, it cannot be doubted that the story serves to reinforce taboos surrounding menstruating women and incest. I do wonder, however, whether this story derives its power from its articulation of the familiar and accepted notions and practices of Wintu culture.[6] On the contrary, I would say, the story speaks more eloquently about the fears that give rise to cultural taboos than it does about the taboos themselves. In its representation of the perversions of oral longings, it speaks more insistently of desires that cannot be satisfied than it does of cultural resolutions of age-old problems. Indeed, the story seems to suggest that the cultural taboos surrounding female sexuality are as destructive to the culture as the desires they are designed to repress, since they depend in large measure upon the female's conspiratorial acceptance of the need to conceal female sexuality and, thereby, a fundamental ingredient in female identity.

Incest taboos similar to those of the Wintus can be found in many cultures. This is not to say that all cultures enforce incest taboos in like fashion; it means simply that we recognize something fundamentally human in any effort to repress incestuous desires. More important than our recognition of similarity, however, is our recognition of the ubiquity of human failure. We can locate in all structures designed to conceal such longings the inadequacy of doing so, since the very existence of these structures offers poignant reminders of the needs they are designed to mask.[7]

The Wintus address the issue of incest in culturally idiosyncratic ways that provide the basis for cross-cultural dialogue, but this dialogue suggests resolutions that may be at best only latent in many Western cultures. The vagina dentata motif prevalent in much pictorial art of the twentieth century offers a case in point. We are more likely to perceive castration anxiety as the motive for representations of orally aggressive females than we are to recognize the projection of an entire culture's desire to consume the female body. Our story, on the other hand, suggests that, for the Wintus, pre-oedipal longings sit much nearer the surface than they do for modern Western culture. Western culture has, in a sense, allowed its substitution, the orally aggressive female, to function as if it were the thing itself, the desire to incorporate the female body at the earliest stages of development.

Unlike depictions of monstrous women who are compelled to castrate as they devour, the Wintu Rolling Head Loon Woman is not introduced as a gaping-mouthed, shark-toothed female. The story begins with a sister who loves her brother and who wishes to play with him as, we might imagine, she has done many times before. The onset of adolescence, however, brings about a recoding of behavior so that what was once play can no longer be viewed as such. The behavior associated with play has become a "bother" to the elder brother. Lying in his bed, tickling him, sitting on him—all these are indications that something is wrong with the younger sister.

That there is lack of consensus over what constitutes "bother" is clear when the elder sister asks the younger, "Why do you always bother my younger brother?" and she replies, "I never bother him." Unless we are meant to divine that the younger sister lies about her behavior—and I see no reason why we should—we are left to conclude that that behavior in and of itself does not constitute "bother"; rather, bother is dependent upon context. As a matter of fact, the narrative does not impute to the younger sister any malevolent wishes toward the brother or the rest of her family. What she does, she does because it is pleasurable. Her sole motive is to enjoy these pleasures, not to cause harm to others. This is true even to the point of devouring herself. She devours her own body because her "blood tasted good" and because "she wanted to eat her flesh."

The parallels between the blood that drips from the young girl's cut finger and the bloodlike discharge of the menstruating female cannot be overlooked, in part because of the great pleasure she takes in tasting her own blood and in part because of the association that is made in the story between onanism and cannibalism. On one hand, the satisfaction she experiences when tasting her own blood suggests satisfaction with her emerging female sexual identity. She takes pleasure in the new body awareness that accompanies the onset of puberty. On the other hand, the conjunction of onanism and cannibalism suggests some of the uncertainties associated with the pre-oedipal longings on which Klein and Winnicott dwell. The desire the child has to incorporate the breast stems from confusion about the boundaries between child and mother. From the child's point of view, the oral gratifications supplied by the breast are an extension of the body's need, or hunger. The breast satisfies the needs of the body and the child experiences pleasure. It is only when the breast is withdrawn during the weaning process that the child recognizes a need or desire to cannibalize the breast in order to ensure that it is ever present. A certain degree of sadistic pleasure accrues, as well, since by cannibalizing the mother the child can exact some revenge on her for having withdrawn the source of oral and bodily pleasure.

The conflicting needs satisfied by the conjunction of onanism and cannibalism manifest themselves in other ways as well. Because the young girl's experience of pleasure depends so much upon the disappearance of her body, her actions seem too easily to suit the needs of the community at large. The young girl herself experiences no shame and sees no need to conceal her maturing body. Her parents, elder brother, and elder sister, however, compel her to hide her body, first in the menstrual hut and then behind the menstrual apron. The pleasure she takes in devouring her body suggests a willing complicity on her part to incorporate the wish of the family that her body disappear. The fact that the elder sister conveys the family's wishes to her sister suggests a willing complicity on the part of all the women in satisfying the needs of the larger group. The narrative itself satisfies the culture's need to conceal its own anxiety regarding female sexuality behind a grotesque representation of the young girl's delight in her own body.

Paradoxically, it is the conflation of the young girl's pleasure with the wishes of the community that problematizes her status as a monster. We might judge that it is her own insatiable oral needs that transform her into Rolling Head Woman, but we might equally judge that it is the desire of the community to suppress female sexuality that unleashes the oral aggression of the young girl, in which case her aggression serves as a reasonable defense against the culture's wish to deny an essential part of her identity.

I believe, however, that we need not choose between these two possibilities. The young girl is Rolling Head Woman because she has insatiable needs *and* because she wishes to defend herself against the desires of the community. In order to make this point clear, we must remember that the nursing child has no gender identity that could be differentiated from the mother's. The mother functions as an extension of the child. As a consequence, from the point of view of the child, mother and child form an undifferentiated whole. In her role as adolescent in the story, the young girl represents all undifferentiated children entering the stage of differentiation. Her oral longings symbolize those of each member of the culture. Her isolation at the onset of adolescence represents that experienced by all members of the group. Moreover, her aggression constitutes a defense against separation and isolation similar to that experienced by each Wintu somewhere in a less verbally articulate past. She wishes to be joined to the group, and she satisfies this need by devouring the group. Culture, however, dictates that she join the group in a less anarchic fashion. Conforming to cultural practice, in this case accepting the taboos regarding menstruation and incest, offers each member of the group a symbolic mode of incorporation. The story suggests that the Wintus have not resolved for themselves the inevitable tension and resulting confusion about identity that distinguishes swallowing the group and being swallowed by the group.

Clues to why the narrative places the young girl in the position of transmitting this psycho-sociological information may be found in this story as well. Among the many striking features of the story is the number of siblings in this Wintu family: two boys and two girls. They function as units, the women being called upon to shift alliances from gender to birth order as the needs of the story dictate. The elder boy and girl speak in a single voice in their condemnation of the younger sister's seemingly inappropriate advances to the elder brother. On the other hand, the sisters form a unit when gender-specific cultural practices are foregrounded. Such restructuring of alliances suggests that women can be asked to endorse behaviors that undermine same-gender alliances for the sake of preserving cultural identity. Women are called upon to condemn female behavior that undermines the integrity of the culture. This is not a demand placed upon the men in the story. Though they form alliances with women, they never do so at the risk of sacrificing their identities as members of the group made up of Wintu males.

The actions of the father and younger brother help illustrate this point. The father's voice is distinguished from that of the choral "they" only once in the story. This occurs after we are told that the family "went above empty-handed," and the father says, "Oh, dear, our own child has orphaned us." The empty hands of the family refer in part, no doubt, to the loss of material possessions that coincides with their hasty retreat from the monstrous daughter. Nevertheless, empty hands are also associated with the loss of the elder son, and the patriarchal voice draws attention to this fact. The loss of the valued son brings much more grief to the family than the loss of the (undervalued?) daughter. Her loss, which is represented in a number of different ways in the story—through her exile from the earth lodge, through the concealment of her female sexuality, and only finally through her transformation into Rolling Head Woman—occurs without comment on the part of the family members. The elder sister vows to find her younger brother but not to redeem the younger sister.

In addition, the family—and the natural world at large—solicits the younger brother's help in the rebirth of the elder brother. I may be guilty of a too formulaic reading if I say that the cultural impulse toward regeneration and renewal is evident in the introduction of the incidents associated with the lake. A symbolic womb, as it were, provides the setting for the regeneration of the elder brother and is the site, moreover, of the clandestine plotting of the elder sister and younger brother. The rebirth of the elder brother depends upon the younger son's piercing Rolling Head Loon Woman and the elder sister's cooking of the heart, clearly activities deemed gender-appropriate by the Wintus. We can only speculate as to whether or not these activities also refer to intercourse and gestation, because we have too little information about Wintu language itself. If they do, they offer clear evidence of the sublimated incestuous desires of the other siblings.

At every juncture of the story we are given invaluable information about Wintu culture, and the story inevitably functions as a carrier of this information. The narrative itself, however, serves other, more important ends as well. Narrative configures cultural information in such a way as to recreate the needs and desires that give rise to cultural practices. In doing so, narratives demonstrate the anxieties surrounding any culture's answers to its most pressing questions. Even though cultural practices may prevail and have the consent of a majority of a culture's members, they may at the same time be viewed as only contingent solutions to a cultural dilemma or problem. They constitute solutions to problems, but they are solutions that members of the community recognize as being conditional or even flawed. The cultural practices associated with incest and menstruation cannot control the desires they attempt to contain. They offer, at best, partial solutions that work ineffectively, and sometimes not at all. Were this not clear in other ways, it certainly is clear from the contamination that infects the cultural hero (a representation of the culture itself). The Wintu culture's inability to defend itself against the threat from within results in a culture aware that it might not "live very long."

It is the unmanageability of certain taboos and the feared disintegration of culture itself that the Wintus examine every time they tell or listen to this story. In other words, the story not only functions to indoctrinate boys and girls in the ways of Wintu culture but serves as an acceptable outlet for criticism of the indoctrination (and culture-making) process itself. The Wintus understand, if only unconsciously, that cultural practices alone do not guarantee the survival of Wintu culture; there are some longings that cannot be reasoned away, no matter how rhetorically successful the argument against them.

Notes

1. Kenneth Burke, "Freud—and the Analysis of Poetry," in *The Philosophy of Literary Form: Studies in Symbolic Action,* rev. ed. (New York: Random House, 1961), p. 229.

144 / LINDA AINSWORTH

This article originally appeared as Linda Ainsworth, "If Texts Are Prayers, What Do Wintu Want?" in *American Indian Persistence and Resurgence,* ed. Karl Kroeber (Durham NC: Duke University Press, 1994). Reprinted with permission.

2. The object relations theorists I have in mind are Melanie Klein, especially her "Criminal Tendencies in Normal Children" (1927), "Love, Guilt, and Reparation" (1937), "On the Theory of Anxiety and Guilt" (1948), and "Envy and Gratitude" (1957), all reprinted in *The Writings of Melanie Klein* (New York: Free Press, 1975), 1:170–85, 1:306–43, 2:25–42, and 2:176–235; and Donald Winnicott, most especially his *Playing and Reality* (New York: Routledge, 1989).

3. Peter Brooks, *Body Works: Objects of Desire in Modern Narrative* (Cambridge MA: Harvard University Press, 1993), p. 7. Brooks is paraphrasing an argument found variously in Klein's writings but well articulated in "Early Stages of the Oedipus Conflict," in *Contributions to Psycho-Analysis, 1921–1945* (London: Hogarth, 1950), pp. 202–26.

4. Winnicott, *Playing and Reality,* pp. 11–15, 100.

5. This story and variants are published in Cora DuBois and Dorothy Demetracoupolou, *Wintu Myths,* University of California Publications in American Archaeology and Ethnology 28 (Berkeley: University of California Press, 1931).

6. Cora DuBois documents practices surrounding the onset of menses in *Wintu Ethnography,* University of California Publications in American Archaeology and Ethnology 36 (Berkeley: University of California Press, 1935).

7. According to Gregorio Kohon, "*What makes sexuality in human beings specifically human is repression,* that is to say, sexuality owes its existence to our unconscious incestuous fantasies. Desire, in human sexuality, is always transgression; and being something that is never completely fulfilled, its object cannot ever offer full satisfaction" (original emphasis). See "Reflections on Dora: The Case of Hysteria," in *The British School of Psychoanalysis: The Independent Tradition,* ed. Gregorio Kohon (New Haven CT: Yale University Press, 1986), p. 371. I take Kohon to mean that because we must repress the desires associated with the mother's breast and transfer desire to a substitute object, recognition of sexuality always carries with it a sense of loss.

The Youth and Maiden Who Played Hide and Seek for Their Life *

Ishyaoí! In Oraíbi the people were living. At the west end of the south row of houses lived a youth. A short distance north-east of the present Honáni kiva lived a maiden. One day the youth went down to the west side of the mesa to watch his father's fields.

---

*H. R. Voth, *The Traditions of the Hopi,* Publications of the Field Columbian Museum 8 (Chicago, 1905), pp. 16–41.

As he passed the house of the maiden she asked where he was going. "I am going to watch my father's fields," he said. "May I not go along?" she asked. "Yes," he said, thinking that she was only joking, and passed on. She wrapped up some fresh píki rolls and followed the youth. "So you have come," he said to her by way of greeting when she had arrived. "Yes," she said, and opening her blanket showed him her píki, which they ate together. "Let us play hide and seek now," she said, "and the one who is found four times shall be killed." "All right," he replied, "you hide first because you wanted it." "No, you hide first," she said, and so finally they agreed that the girl would go and hide first. "But you must not look after me," she warned the youth, and spread her blanket (ushímni) over him.

She then ran through the growing corn and finally hid under some cornstalks. As soon as she had hidden she called out "tow." The young man then commenced to hunt her but could not find her. Finally he said: "I cannot find you, come out." So she came out and they went back to the place where they had eaten, and the youth then went to hide himself, covering up the girl with her blanket. He hid under a saltbush. Having hidden, he called out, "tow," whereupon the girl hunted for him and found him. Hereupon they again returned, the youth was covered up and the girl again went among the growing corn to hide. Finding a large corn-stalk, she pulled out the tassel, crawled into the opening and put the tassel in again. She then signaled to the youth, and he came and looked for her. Following her tracks he found that she had been running through the corn-field. So he hunted throughout the corn-field and then at the edge among the herbs and grasses, but could not find her. Finally he noticed that her tracks seemed to come to an end near a large corn-stalk, but he could not find her anywhere. Finally he called out, "I cannot find you, where are you?" "Here I am," she replied, and throwing out the corn-tassel she jumped out. So for the second time he had failed to find her.

They again returned to the edge of the field, the girl now covering herself up. The youth now, as he went through the field, was thinking, "Where shall I hide? It is time that she does not find me again." As he passed along the edge of the field he heard a voice. "Listen to me," some one said. "Come up here. I have pity on you. One time she has already found you, and she will certainly find you again." This was the Sun. Hereupon the latter threw down a rainbow upon which the youth climbed to the Sun, who hid him behind his back saying, "Here she will not find you." So the girl followed his tracks all through the field, and went to the edge of the field to a small knoll, but could not find him. She followed them again throughout the field and returned to the same place. By this time she was puzzled where he could be. Her hair whorls were hanging down out of shape. She was thinking and thinking where he might be. Finally she pressed a few drops of milk out of her breast, examined the drops in her hand, and seeing the sun reflected in them, she discovered the boy behind him. She at once said, "Aha, there you are; I have found you. Come down."

The youth now again covered himself up and the girl went to hide away the third time. But this time the youth lifted up a corner of the covering and watched her, in which direction she went. When he followed her tracks throughout the corn-field he could not find her. Her tracks led to a patch of watermelons and squashes, but as the runners covered the ground he could not find her there. He returned to the corn-field and hunted, but not finding her anywhere he again followed her tracks to the water-melon patch. Finally he gave up in despair and called out, "I cannot find you, come out." She then burst open a watermelon, saying, "Here I am, and you did not find me," and came out.

The youth by this time became unhappy. They again returned and the maiden covering herself up, the youth went to hide away, but was very unhappy. Running through the corn-field and along its edge, he all at once heard a voice. "Where are you going? I have pity on you. You come in here," and looking down he saw a small hole by the side of a small corn-stalk. It was the house of Spider Woman. This he entered and she quickly spun some web across the opening. The girl again went to hunt for the youth. Running through the corn-field repeatedly, she finally traced his tracks to the edge of the corn-field, but could not find him anywhere. She then drew forth from her bosom a mirror made from a quartz crystal. Through this she hunted first upward, hoping to find him somewhere above again, but failed to find him. She then turned it downward and all at once saw the opening of the Spider's hole reflected in it. "Come out," she at once called out, "I have found you. You are in there." Spider Woman said, "Well, you will have to go out, she has found you." He was very dejected by this time because there was only one chance for him left; but he came out.

For the fourth time the girl went to hide away. The youth again lifted up a corner of the covering and looked after her and saw that she was again running towards the watermelon patch. On one side of the corn-field was a ditch and as it had rained shortly before, there was some water in this ditch and a number of tadpoles were in this water. The girl crossed the watermelon patch, went into the ditch, entered the water and turned into a tadpole. The boy again went in search of the girl, following her tracks through the corn-field and through the watermelon patch down to the ditch, but failed to find her. He returned and hunted throughout the field, and being very tired, he returned to the water, stooped down and drank some. He was very sad by this time, but he hunted once more. Finally he again followed her tracks to the edge of the water, and knowing that she must be there somewhere, he called out, "I cannot find you, just come out," and immediately she emerged from the water and said, "I was here when you were drinking water and I looked right at you." He then remembered that a tadpole had looked up out of the water when he was drinking, but he, of course, never thought that that could be the maiden.

So they returned again to the same place, and as they went back the youth was very much discouraged. "Only one chance left for me," he thought, "where shall I hide that she will not find me?" After the girl had covered herself he again went away. Passing the house of Spider Woman, the latter said to him, "Alas! where are you going? You go there a little to the east to your uncle, the Áhü (a species of worm that lives in rotten wood); he lives in the takáchi (a temporary shelter) and maybe he will hide you." So the youth went there and when he arrived there called out, "My uncle, put me in there." So the Áhü pulled out a loose knot from one of the corner poles, which was that of a piñon-tree. This post was hollow, and into this the Áhü put the youth, closing up the opening after he had entered. So the girl went and hunted for the youth, following his tracks through the corn-field, and found that he had been going up and down and back and forth, and finally she tracked them to the shelter. Arriving at this place she hunted, but at first could not find him. She then put the tips of her right hand fingers, one after another, into her mouth, wet them slightly, then pressed the point of her forefinger into her right ear, and immediately she heard the youth in his hiding place and told him to come out, as she had found him.

They then returned to their place again, but the girl said: "Let us now return again to the shelter where I found you." So they returned and sat down close to the shelter on the north side. The girl hereupon dug a hole close to one of the corner posts and then said to the youth: "I have beaten you, I have beaten you. You take off your shirt." He did so. It was a blue shirt such as the Hopi used to wear. "Now take off your beads," she said, and, not knowing what she intended to do, he did so. She hereupon grabbed him by the hair, jerked out a knife from behind her belt, bent him over the hole that she had made, and cut his throat, letting the blood run into the hole. She then closed up this hole, dug another one somewhat to the north and dragged the body to it, burying it in this grave.

Hereupon she took the shirt and the beads with her and went home. When the young man did not return to his home his parents became worried and inquired at the maiden's house. "We thought you both had gone to our field to watch," they said. "Do you not know where Kwavúhü is?" "Yes," she said, "we were there together, but he drove me away, and I do not know where he is." So the parents were very sad. They had killed a sheep shortly before, but as they were so sorry they ate very little of the meat, and so the flies came in and ate of the meat. One time the woman was driving the flies off with a broom and one of them said, "Why do you drive me away when I eat your meat? I suck some of this meat and then I shall go and hunt your child." Hereupon the woman desisted and the flies then sucked of the meat. "Yes," the woman then said to the fly, "our boy went to watch the fields and he never came back. If you can, you go and hunt him and find him for me." So the Fly flew away to the corn-field and found very many tracks. Following them all over the field, she finally tracked them to the shelter where the young man had been killed. Flying around here she soon discovered traces of the blood, and opening the hole she found blood in it. She sucked some of this blood and went a little farther north and there found the grave. She then sucked up all the blood from the first opening and injected it into the body and then waited. Soon the heart of the youth began to beat and after a little while he raised up, shaking his head slightly. "Have you woken up?" the Fly said. "Yes," he answered, "but I am very thirsty." "There is some water over there in the ditch," the Fly said, "go there and drink and then we shall return to your house." So he went there and quenched his thirst and then they returned to the house of his parents. These were now very happy when they saw the child. The Fly then said to the parents, "The shirt and beads of your boy are at the maiden's house. Let him go over there and then see what she says, whether she will be glad or not, and then let him ask for his shirt and beads, and when she gives him the shirt let him shake it at her, and then when he gets the beads he must shake them, too."

The mother then said to her son, "All right, you go over to the house." But the Fly continued, "She will probably spread food before you, she will offer you píki rolls, but do not eat them." So he went over there. When the girl saw him she exclaimed, "Ih (with a rising inflection), have you come?" "Yes," he said, "I have come." "Sit down," she said to him, and at once went into another room and got some food, which she placed before him. "I am not hungry; I have come for my shirt and my beads. I think you brought them with you when you came." "Yes, I have them here, and of course I shall give them to you." She hereupon went into a room and when she opened the door the young man looked in and saw that she was very wealthy. She had a great many things there that she had taken from the youths whom she had killed. When she brought out his things he took them and shook them at her and said, "Yes, these are mine, these are the ones." Hereupon he left the house, but the Fly had in the meanwhile told his parents that they should go over to the girl's house also and meet their son there, so they met in front of the house and waited there. While they were standing there they heard a noise in the house, some clapping and shaking. When the young man had shaken his shirt and the beads at the girl, an evil charm had entered her and she was changed into "Tíhkuy Wuhti" (child protruding woman). She entered an inner room and came out dressed in a white robe. Her hair was now tied up like that of a married woman, but her face and clothes were all bloody. While she had put on this costume the noise and rattle in the room where the costumes of the slain youths were had continued, and these costumes, which it seems consisted mostly of buckskins, rabbit skins, etc., had assumed the shape of deer, antelope and rabbits, and these now dashed out of the room and left the house. The girl tried to keep them and was angry, but could not stop them. She grabbed the last one, however, and wiping her hand over her genitalia she rubbed this hand over the face of the antelope, twisted his nose, rubbed his horns, etc., and then let him run. She then turned to the people who had assembled outside of the house and said, "After this you shall have great difficulty in hunting these animals. If you had let them alone here they would have remained close by, and you would have had no difficulty in slaying them." She thereupon also left the house and disappeared with the game. Ever after she lived along the Little Colorado River, where also for a long time the deer and antelope abounded. And this is the reason why it is so difficult to approach and kill this game. The Tíhkuy Wuhti having rubbed her own odor over the nose and face of that antelope, these antelopes now smell the odor of people from a far distance, and so it is very difficult to approach them. The Tíhkuy Wuhti is said to still live at the Little Colorado River, and the Hopi claim to have seen her, still wrapped up in the white robe, and all covered with blood. She controls the game, and hunters make prayer-offerings to her of turquoise and nakwákwosis stained in red ochre like that used in the Snake ceremony. These prayer-offerings, however, are always deposited in the night.

Selected Bibliography

A highly selective bibliography of works useful for introductory study of traditional American Indian stories.

Basso, Keith Hamilton. *Stalking with Stories and Other Essays on Western Apache Language and Culture.* Tucson: University of Arizona Press, 1990.
Reprinting of marvelously informative essays on purposes and techniques of Indian storytelling.

Bauman, Richard. *Verbal Art as Performance.* 1977. Reprint, Prospect Heights IL: Waveland, 1984.
Illuminating analysis of storytelling as performative event; attached essays by other scholars add to the book's value.

Bierhorst, John, ed. *Four Masterworks of American Indian Literature.* Tucson: University of Arizona Press, 1974.
Includes edited and annotated versions of the Iroquois "Ritual of Condolence" and the Navaho "Night Chant" ceremony.

Bright, William. *American Indian Linguistics and Literature.* New York: Mouton, 1984.
Contains useful comments on and applications of Hymes's and Tedlock's methods in reference to Coyote stories.

Brumble, H. David. *American Indian Autobiography.* Berkeley: University of California Press, 1988.
Valuable survey of this vast and complex genre.

Clements, William M., and Frances M. Malpezzi, eds. *Native American Folklore, 1879–1979: An Annotated Bibliography.* Athens OH: Swallow, 1984.
Most complete and accurate source of information on both criticism and collections of American Indian stories.

Dauenhauer, Nora Marks, and Richard Dauenhauer, eds. *Haa Shuká, Our Ancestors: Tlingit Oral Narratives.* Seattle: University of Washington Press, 1987.
Unusually sensitive translations of Indian stories with detailed and useful annotations.

Dundes, Alan. "Texture, Text, and Context." *Southern Folklore Quarterly* 28, no. 4 (1964): 251–65.

Seminal essay for analyses of oral storytelling.

Fine, Elizabeth C. *The Folklore Text: From Performance to Print*. Bloomington: University of Indiana Press, 1984.

Comprehensive explanations of recent methods of analysis of oral materials.

Hymes, Dell H. *"In Vain I Tried to Tell You": Essays in Native American Ethnopoetics*. Philadelphia: University of Pennsylvania Press, 1981.

Essential collection of elaborate analyses, the basis for Hymes's influence on new scholarship treating "poetic" patterning in American Indian stories and songs.

Jacobs, Melville. *The Content and Style of an Oral Literature: Clackamas Chinook Texts*. Viking Fund Publications in Anthropology 26. Chicago: University of Chicago Press, 1959.

———. *The People Are Coming: Analyses of Clackamas Chinook Myths and Tales*. Seattle: University of Washington Press, 1960.

Detailed studies of literary qualities; Hymes used these as a starting point for his pioneering work in ethnopoetics.

Jahner, Elaine A. "Cognitive Style in Oral Literature." *Language and Style* 16 (1982): 32–51.

Important discussion of form in Lakota storytelling.

Kroeber, Karl. "Religion, Literary Art, and the Retelling of Myth." *Religion and Literature* 26, no. 1 (1994): 9–30.

Assessment of the significance of an early twentieth-century Indian's spectacular revision of a major Lakota myth.

———. *Retelling/Rereading: The Fate of Storytelling in Modern Times*. New Brunswick NJ: Rutgers University Press, 1992.

Includes extensive use of traditional Native American stories to illustrate principles of narrative art.

Lankford, George E., comp. and ed. *Native American Legends: Southeastern Tales from the Natchez, Caddo, Biloxi, Chickasaw, and Other Nations*. Intro. W. K. McNeil. Little Rock AR: August House, 1987.

Usefully annotated collection of stories from the Southeast, a region normally underrepresented in collections.

Ramsey, Jarold, ed. *Coyote Was Going There: Indian Literature of the Oregon Country*. Seattle: University of Washington Press, 1977.

Fullest and best annotated collection from the Northwest.

———. *Reading the Fire: Essays in the Traditional Literatures of the Far West*. Lincoln: University of Nebraska Press, 1983.

A gathering of brilliant essays by the most literarily sensitive of commentators on Native American myths and tales.

Schoolcraft, Henry Rowe. *The Myth of Hiawatha and Other Oral Legends, Mythologies, and Allegories of the North American Indians.* 1856. Reprint, Millwood NY: Kraus, 1971.
Reprint of major works of one of the earliest "scientific" collectors of Indian lore.

Sherzer, Joel, and Anthony C. Woodberry, eds. *Native American Discourse: Poetics and Rhetoric.* Cambridge: Cambridge University Press, 1987.
Six valuably detailed commentaries on specific texts by professional linguists inspired by Dell Hymes.

Swann, Brian, ed. *Coming to Light: Contemporary Translations of the Native American Literatures of North America.* New York: Random House, 1994.
Excellent anthology with a contextualizing critical commentary by the translator of each selection.

———. *Smoothing the Ground: Essays on Native American Oral Literature.* Berkeley: University of California Press, 1983.
Large collection of critical essays on a variety of aspects of Indian storytelling.

Tedlock, Dennis. *Finding the Center: Narrative Poetry of the Zuni Indians.* New York: Dial, 1972. Reprint, Lincoln: University of Nebraska Press, 1978.
Essential pioneering work in the presentation of Native American storytelling as artistically significant performance.

———. *The Spoken Word and the Work of Interpretation.* Philadelphia: University of Pennsylvania Press, 1983.
Invaluable collection of critical essays delineating the performative artistry of oral myth telling.

Thompson, Stith, ed. *Tales of the North American Indians.* Bloomington: University of Indiana Press, 1966.
A wide variety of myths from many sources, elaborately indexed and cross-referenced.

Vecsey, Christopher. *Imagine Ourselves Richly: Mythic Narrative of North American Indians.* San Francisco: Harper, 1991.
Studies of several longer myths and ceremonies.

Vizenor, Gerald. "*Trickster Discourse*: Comic Holotropes and Language Games." In *Narrative Chance: Postmodern Discourse on Native American Indian Literatures,* ed. Gerald Vizenor, 187–211. Albuquerque: University of New Mexico Press, 1989.

Sophisticated commentaries on the nature and function of the Trickster in Indian cultures, with useful references to earlier commentators.

Waldman, Carl. *Atlas of the North American Indian.* New York: Facts on File, 1985.
Splendid maps, good text describing pre- and postcontact migrations, wars, and major cultural and social developments.

Washburn, Wilcomb E., ed. *The Indian and the White Man.* Garden City NY: Doubleday, Anchor, 1964.
Excellent collection of documents pertaining to Indian-white relations from time of European contact.

———. *The Indian in America.* New York: Harper, 1975.
Cogent study of causes and results of difficulties in Indian-white relations.

Witherspoon, Gary. *Language and Art in the Navajo Universe.* Ann Arbor: University of Michigan Press, 1977.
Important analysis of the relation of language to culture.

The Contributors

Linda Ainsworth is Assistant Dean of Student Affairs at Columbia College.

Dell Hymes is Commonwealth Professor of Anthropology and English at the University of Virginia. His books include *Essays in the History of Linguistic Anthropology, Foundations in Sociolinguistics: An Ethnographic Approach, Language in Education: Ethnolinguistic Essays, Reinventing Anthropology,* and *"In vain I tried to tell you": Essays in Native American Ethnopoetics.*

Karl Kroeber is Mellon Professor in the Humanities in the Department of English and Comparative Literature at Columbia University. His recent books include *Retelling/Rereading: The Fate of Storytelling in Modern Times* and *Ecological Literary Criticism.* He is currently finishing a study of the imaginative forms of Native American myths.

Jarold Ramsey is Professor of English at the University of Rochester. His books include *Coyote Was Going There: Indian Literature from the Oregon Country* and *Reading the Fire: Essays in the Traditional Indian Literatures of the Far West* (Nebraska, 1983).

Tacheeni Scott is Professor of Biology at California State University, Northridge. He purposely incorporates Native American principles of research into his teaching.

Dennis Tedlock is James H. McNulty Professor in the Department of English and Research Professor of Anthropology at the State University of New York at Buffalo and Coeditor of *American Anthropologist.* His books include *Popol Vuh: The Mayan Book of the Dawn of Life, Breath on the Mirror: Mythic Voices and Visions of the Living Maya, The Dialogic Emergence of Culture,* and *Finding the Center: Narrative Poetry of the Zuni Indians* (Nebraska, 1978).

Barre Toelken is Professor of English and History at Utah State University, where he is Director of both the graduate program in American Studies and the interdisciplinary Folklore Program. He has served as Editor of the *Journal of American Folklore* and his books include *The Dynamics of Folklore, Ghosts and the Japanese: Cultural Experience in Japanese Death Legends* (with Michiko Iwasaka), and *Morning Dew and Roses: Nuance, Metaphor and Meaning in Folksongs.*

Index